Power-Glide Spanish Junior 1

Power-Glide Spanish Junior 1
2005 Edition

Project Coordinator: James Blair

Development Manager: Dave Higginbotham

Editor: Debi Barrett

Editorial Assistants: Debbie Haws, Erik D. Holley, Kari Feldhaus, Nancy Van Erp

Voice Talent: Carlos Amado, Edgar Zurita

Layout & Design: Erik D. Holley

Illustrators: Heather Monson, Apryl Robertson

Course Writers: Kari Feldhaus, Nancy Van Erp

Story Writers: Heather Monson, Kristen Knight

Recording Engineers: Wade Chamberlain, Edgar Zurita

© 2005 Power-Glide Language Courses, Inc. All rights reserved.
Printed in the United States of America
ISBN: 1-58204-262-4

No part of this publication may be reproduced, stored in a retrieval system or transmitted in any form or by any means, electronic, mechanical, photocopying, recording, scanning, or otherwise without the prior written permission of Power-Glide.

Power-Glide Language Courses, Inc.
1682 W 820 N, Provo, UT 84601

www.power-glide.com

Contents

Introduction 1

Junior 1

    Module 1.1 9

        Section 1.1.1   **Arrival in Spain** 11

Activity 1	How Will Learning Spanish Help Me?	14
Activity 2	Where is Spanish Spoken?	16
Activity 3	Common Greetings and Phrases	19
Activity 4	Animal Vocabulary	22
Activity 5	What's in a Name?	26
Activity 6	*Los animales*	29
Activity 7	What is Your Animal Like?	33
Activity 8	*La gallinita roja:* Part I	37
Activity 9	Animal Culture	41
Section 1.1.1	Quiz	45

        Section 1.1.2   **Legend of the Sword** 49

Activity 10	Journal	53
Activity 11	*En la granja*	57
Activity 12	Farms	60
Activity 13	*La gallinita roja:* Part II	64
Activity 14	Present Tense	68
Activity 15	*La granja*	71
Activity 16	What Would Your Farm Be Like?	75
Activity 17	Numbers and Animals	77
Activity 18	Cultural Music	82
Section 1.1.2	Quiz	86

    Module 1.2 91

        Section 1.2.1   **A Flamenco Festival** 93

Activity 19	Journal	95
Activity 20	Jobs	98
Activity 21	*Trabajos*	103
Activity 22	Other Words on the Job	106
Activity 23	Job Culture	110
Activity 24	*La gallinita roja:* Part III	112
Activity 25	*El trabajo:* Matching	116
Activity 26	On the Job	121
Activity 27	Create a Story	124
Section 1.2.1	Quiz	126

CONTENTS — POWER-GLIDE SPANISH JUNIOR I

Section 1.2.2		**A Few Close Calls**	131
	Activity 28	Journal	133
	Activity 29	*El teléfono*	137
	Activity 30	Numbers and Telling Time	141
	Activity 31	*Hablando por teléfono*	146
	Activity 32	*El periodista en el teléfono*	149
	Activity 33	*El patito feo:*	
parte I			154
	Activity 34	*El Futuro:* Making Plans	159
	Activity 35	Create a Phone Conversation	163
	Activity 36	*Leyendo:* Practice Your Reading Skills	166
	Section 1.2.2	Quiz	169
Module 1.3			**175**
Section 1.3.1		**Escape from the University**	177
	Activity 37	Journal	179
	Activity 38	Daily Routine	182
	Activity 39	What's Happening Today?	186
	Activity 40	Reflexive Verbs	189
	Activity 41	*El patito feo:*	
parte II			192
	Activity 42	The U.S. and Spanish-Speaking Countries	197
	Activity 43	My Day	200
	Activity 44	More Reflexive Verbs and Review	205
	Activity 45	Make Posters: What Happens When?	207
	Section 1.3.1	Quiz	209
Section 1.3.2		**The Rest of the Clue**	213
	Activity 46	Journal	215
	Activity 47	*Las meriendas*	217
	Activity 48	*Los huevos de oro*	223
	Activity 49	Let's Go on a Trip!	227
	Activity 50	*En la granja de Mario*	232
	Activity 51	Past Tense	235
	Activity 52	*Cinco de Mayo*	238
	Activity 53	More Past Tense	241
	Activity 54	*Repaso*	243
	Section 1.3.2	Quiz	247

Appendix A • Student Answer Keys ... 252

Appendix B • Scope and Sequence ... 266

Appendix C • Index of Marginalia ... 271

Introduction

Using This Course

Welcome to Power-Glide Foreign Language Courses! You hold in your hands a very powerful and effective language learning tool. Power-Glide courses are designed so that individual students working alone can use them just as well as students in classrooms. However, before starting, we'd like to offer a few tips and explanations to help you get the most from your learning experience.

The course is divided into modules, sections, and activities. Each page has a tab denoting how it fits into the course structure, and students can use these tabs to navigate their way through the course.

Each module has two sections, and each section begins with a page or two of adventure story, ends with a section quiz, and has several language activities in between.

Sections are followed by quizzes which we encourage students to use to solidify their mastery of the materials presented in the activities. These quizzes are very helpful for students seeking credit for their course work.

In this course, students will find a variety of different activities. These activities include DiglotWeave™ stories, counting and number activities, storytelling activities, activities designed to build conversational ability, audio-off activities for building reading comprehension, Spanish-only activities for building listening comprehension, and much more. Word puzzles found at the beginning of some sections help the student to think and problem-solve Spanish.

These different activity types accommodate different types of learning, and all are learner-tested and effective. Students will no doubt notice that each activity begins with a new picture. These pictures are drawn from Spanish cultures and countries and are included for students' interest.

How to Use the Appendices

- Appendix A contains student answers for self quizzes and exercises. Students using this appendix will receive immediate feedback on their work.
- Appendix B contains the Scope and Sequence for this course. This appendix outlines the specific language learning objectives for each section and is useful for students seeking credit or teachers looking to schedule curriculum.
- Appendix C is an index of marginalia, or information found in the margins throughout the course.

Students are encouraged to familiarize themselves with these appendices, as they can be valuable resources for finding information quickly.

Getting the Most Out of This Course

- Recognize the audio on and audio off symbols.
- Understand the text.
- Speak and write.

Audio Symbols

The audio-on and audio-off symbols, as mentioned previously, are highlighted bars like those below. Watch for them to know when to use your audio CDs.

When you see this bar, press play on your CD.

When you see this bar, press pause on your CD. Do not push stop. Pausing will allow you to continue the track where you left off, rather than at the beginning of the disc.

Understanding the Text

1. Look over the material and compare the Spanish to the English.
2. Listen to the audio tracks while following the written text.
3. Listen to the audio tracks a couple of times without looking at the written text.
4. Use the pause button to stop the audio for a moment if you want more time to practice.

Speaking

1. Read the story or material out loud in chorus with the audio, and keep the meaning in mind.
2. Turn the audio off, read each sentence out loud in Spanish, and then look away and repeat the same sentence without looking. Think of the meaning.
3. Now cover up the Spanish, look at the first English sentence, and try to say it in Spanish. Check to see if you did it right. Repeat this process for all the sentences in the activity.
4. Play the recording of the text, but pause the audio after each English sentence and say the Spanish yourself.
5. Using notes of key words only, try to say the Spanish sentences without using your activity book. It's okay to put the sentences into your own words, just keep them in Spanish as much as possible.

Writing

To write, just follow the same directions for speaking, but write your sentences instead of speaking them.

Course Conventions

Objectives

Each activity has a shaded box letting learners know what they will learn during the activity.

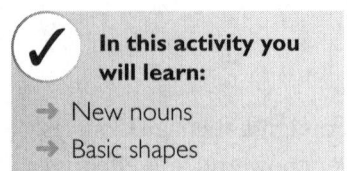

In this activity you will learn:
→ New nouns
→ Basic shapes

Sections also have objectives boxes. These section objectives are drawn from the activity objectives within the section. Appendix B contains a list of all the activity objectives for your convenience when reviewing for quizzes.

Performance Challenges

While optional, students are encouraged to try performance challenges to fill out each activity and reinforce its content. Performance challenge boxes are located at the end of activities and look like this:

Not all activities have performance challenges and some have multiple challenges. Each performance challenge is labeled for use by an individual student or study group. If an activity has multiple performance challenges, the student may choose one or more to work on.

Audio Indicators

Some portions of this course have corresponding audio. The shaded audio boxes at the beginning of sections and selected activities indicate which audio disc and track to use. The sample audio box below indicates that disc 1, track 12 contains the audio for the given activity.

Recall the audio symbols described earlier.

You will use these bars together with the shaded audio box as you move through the course.

Here is a sample scenario for how to use the audio indicators:

- If an activity has audio, you will see the shaded audio box indicating which disc and track to use. In this example, we'll suppose that the audio box indicates disc 1, track 1.
- At the first audio-on bar you reach in the activity, insert audio disc 1 into your CD player and play track 1.
- When you reach the audio-off bar, press *pause*.
- The activity may or may not have more audio. If it does, you will see another audio-on bar. When you reach it, press *play*.
- When you reach another audio-off bar, press *pause* again.
- When you have finished your study session, press *stop* on your CD player.

Tracking Progress

The Table of Contents lists each module, section, and activity in the course with a preceding checkmark circle. To track your progress through the course, place a ✓ in the ○ after you complete a module, section, activity, or section quiz.

The Power-Glide Difference

A Few of the Unique Features of Power-Glide

(And What They Mean To The Learner)

1. **Language specific.** Unlike most language training programs, Power-Glide courses are designed for speakers of specific languages, rather than the "one size fits all" approach. This takes advantage of what each language community knows and doesn't know, avoids wasted effort, and also allows special techniques to address language-specific problems.

2. **Based on up-to-date information/research on linguistics and learning methodology.** While the Power-Glide method is revolutionary, it is based on solid research and the most up-to-date information on the relevant disciplines.

3. **Involves learners in immediate use of the language in real situations.** Power-Glide courses avoid the drudgery of rote memorization of words and rules by immediately involving the learners in practical use of the language in real situations. This keeps interest, confidence, and motivation high.

4. **Uses adventure stories and activities.** From the beginning, the students are involved in an adventure story and activities that keep them engaged.

5. **Uses multiple methods of learning: music, stories, activities, and more.** People have different learning styles. By using various methods, music, stories, etc., everyone's style is addressed and learning is accelerated.

6. **Uses the DiglotWeave™ method.** Students start with familiar stories in their own language and gradually transition word by word, into the new language. The context provides the meaning and thus makes the learning an almost effortless, natural process.

7. **Takes learners from the known to the unknown along the easiest path.** While learning a foreign language can be challenging, it does not need to be brutal. The Power-Glide method guides the learners through the most productive and gentle paths.

8. **Uses memory devices and phonemic approximations.** Learning the right pronunciation and

remembering the words and phrases of another language are greatly facilitated by using memory devices and similar sounding words from the student's own language. This also reduces the "fear" of speaking the new language that many people experience.

9. **Doesn't require teachers.** One of the greatest advantages of Power-Glide courses is the fact that the teacher, parent, or facilitator doesn't need to know the language in order to assist the learner in the process. The one assisting also learns as an unexpected by-product of their teaching others.

10. **Many other linguistic strategies.** The variety of methods used increase motivation, retention, joy of learning, and desire to use the target language.

What People Are Saying About Power-Glide

Stephanie Heese, reviewer, *The Review Corner*:

"Speaking and thinking spontaneously in a foreign language is challenging, but is an important goal that is hard to achieve with traditional programs. In Power-Glide courses, emphasis is not on mechanics and rote learning. This course aims to teach children in a manner that simulates natural language acquisition."

Herbert Horne, linguist:

"Thirty years ago, in Guatemala, I used Dr. Blair's materials and they were the best I had ever seen. Now that I could 'test' the materials with more than 40 students in various classes, I am even more convinced that they are the best language teaching materials in existence today."

Susan Moore, reviewer, *Editor's Choice*:

"Most curriculum developers seem to have forgotten what it was like to sit endlessly in a classroom listening and pretending to be interested in boring subject material, but not Dr. Blair."

Linda Rittner, Director, Pleasant Hill Academy:

"As one who designs educational programs for individual students in our school, I must tell you how impressed I have been with the Power-Glide material. I was able to examine the second year course material for our community college. Your course is more comprehensive!"

Module 1.1

Keep these tips in mind as you progress through this module:
1. Read instructions carefully.
2. Repeat aloud all the Spanish words you hear on the audio CDs.
3. Learn at your own pace.
4. Have fun with the activities and practice your new language skills with others.
5. Record yourself speaking Spanish on tape so you can evaluate your own speaking progress.

Arrival in Spain

Your *buenos amigos*, Tony & Lisa, are spending their summer *vacación* with Grandpa Glen *en España*, and they invited you to come, too. As you emerge from *el aeropuerto en Madrid*, the sun shines warm in *el cielo*, but you don't see Grandpa Glen or his rental *auto* anywhere.

"Let's call him," Tony suggests.

You borrow Lisa's cell phone and key in the contact *número* Grandpa Glen gave you. You get the answering machine. You leave *un mensaje* for Grandpa Glen, then hang up *el teléfono*.

"Let's just get *un taxi* and wait for him at the *Villa Valeria*," you suggest.

Un taxi screeches to a halt *cuando* you flag it. *Los tres* of you pile in with your heavy *equipaje* and hand the taxi driver a slip of *papel* with directions to the *Villa Valeria*.

After almost *una hora en el tráfico*, *el taxi* stops at the gates of a large 17th century *villa* on the outskirts of *Madrid*. The lights of several *policía* cars reflect off the intricate wrought-iron fence that surrounds *la villa*.

Tony pays the cab driver, *y los tres* of you walk wearily toward *la villa*. A police officer—a slim, athletic-looking woman with long, dark *cabello* pulled back in a severe knot—approaches. Grandpa's *amigo*, and the owner *de la villa*, Sophia Valeria stands by the front *puerta* crying and talking with a detective.

"Can I help you? *¿Puedo ayudarles?*" the officer asks.

"I hope so. We're here to meet our *abuelo*. *Se llama* Glen," Tony replies

The officer frowns. "*Soy la Inspector Gutierrez.* Why don't you come inside for *un momento?*"

You leave your *equipaje* in the hall, then follow *la inspectora Gutierrez* to *la cocina*, where dinner is still warm on *la estufa*. As you turn the corner, the smell of *paella* makes your mouth water. Without saying *una palabra*, you all dish up *platos* and start eating the warm *paella*.

"*¿Dónde está nuestro abuelo, Inspector?*" Lisa asks after only her second bite.

La inspectora Gutierrez takes a deep breath and looks you each in the *ojos*. "*Su abuelo* has been kidnapped."

"What!" Tony exclaims.

SECTION 1.1.1

✓ **In this section you will:**

→ Read about several reasons for learning Spanish.

→ Learn about Spanish-speaking countries.

→ Listen to and practice saying Spanish greetings and phrases.

→ Learn to identify the Spanish names of animals.

→ Recognize the differences between English and Spanish names.

→ Test your knowledge of animals and verbs.

→ Learn how to use descriptive adjectives.

→ Understand the Spanish words and phrases in the story of "The Little Red Hen."

→ Read about animals living in Spanish-speaking countries.

 Disc 1   Track 1

"Kidnapped? No! Why?" Lisa says all at once.

La inspectora hesitates, then begins, "Well, Lisa, we believe your grandfather was kidnapped so that his captors could use his expertise in tracking down an ancient artifact. This artifact, in the hands of the wrong *personas*, could cause a lot of death and *destrucción*."

"What it is?" you ask.

"I can't go into that right now," *la inspectora* hedges. "We have several teams trying to track it down before your grandfather's captors reach it. Should the kidnappers find it first… who knows what will happen to *España*? *¿Quién sabe que va a pasar* to the world?"

"Well, then what are we waiting for?" asks Lisa. "Let's go find this artifact, and Grandpa!"

La inspectora laughs and rubs Lisa's hair. "I wish you could *ayudarnos*," *la inspectora* Gutierrez says. "*Pero no.* You kids must stay *aquí* where it is safe."

"*Nuestro abuelo* must have left a clue," Tony protests. "*Por lo menos*, you should let us look at it."

La inspectora sits looking at Tony for several moments. Then, suddenly, she stands up and takes Tony by the arm. "*Quizás* you can *ayudar*, for *unos momentos* at least," she says. "Please, come with me. *Por favor, vengan conmigo.*"

Upstairs, several *policías* are taking *notas* and collecting *evidencia* in a spare bedroom. As you move past *la puerta*, your faces drop, and your hearts sink. The room is turned upside down. Even the mattress is in shreds, and small smudges of blood mark the walls near the windows.

"Now, if *ésto es* too *difícil* for you kids to see, we can go downstairs again," *la inspectora* tells you.

Tony shakes his head resolutely. "Did you collect any clues, like receipts, ticket stubs, everyday items that might not be so 'everyday' with a closer look?" he presses.

La inspectora Gutierrez pulls the three of you into an adjoining *sala* where items are untidily piled on *una mesa*.

"Have these been fingerprinted yet?" you ask.

"*Sí*, they have. You can touch them," answers the *inspectora*.

After several *minutos* of searching, you, Tony, and Lisa decide that searching might be more *productivo* if you had a better idea of what to look for. In the past, Grandpa Glen has often used language to hide clues in plain sight. If that is still the case, then a bit of studying should get you on the right path to finding him. Basic greetings, names, and descriptions will definitely be useful, and since Grandpa Glen had a lot of animal pictures on display in the room, you decide you'd better study some animal names in Spanish as well, in case one of the pictures has a clue.

How Will Learning Spanish Help Me?

ACTIVITY

✓ **In this activity you will:**

→ Read about several reasons for learning Spanish.

Refrán

Here is a *refrán* for you to learn. A *refrán* is a Spanish saying. Practice saying this one out loud and use it today in a conversation.

En boca cerrada no entran moscas.
Literal translation: Flies don't enter a closed mouth.
Meaning: Silence is golden.

When you use your new *refrán*, people will probably ask you what it means. You will then have the perfect opportunity to share your knowledge of Spanish with them. You will find the meaning translates but each word doesn't. That is a good way to look at learning a new language. Rather than learning a new word for every word you know in your language, you need to learn ideas in the new language so you can speak in the style of the language. Look for more *refranes* in the future!

So you've decided to embark on the exciting adventure of learning a second language. Congratulations! Maybe you've had friends or relatives ask, "Why do you want to learn Spanish?" You might have said, "I think it will be fun." Or, "I want to travel all over the world someday." Or, "It's a beautiful language." There are many reasons to learn Spanish and it's time to take a look at some of them.

- Spanish is the official language of Spain, Mexico, and several countries throughout Central America, South America, and the Caribbean. In addition, Spanish is the second most commonly spoken language in the United States.

- Each Hispanic country is a fascinating world just waiting to be discovered! Wouldn't you like to travel to one of these countries, especially if you could speak the native language and communicate with the people you meet? You can't expect them to speak English to you when you are a visitor to their country. If you learn to speak Spanish, you will be able to meet and become friends with people from other countries.

- Remember that when you study a language, you also study the culture of those who speak it. It is exciting to learn more about the food, clothing, music, literature, art, holidays, and many other cultural aspects of the Spanish-speaking people. You will find that traditions are very important in the Hispanic world.

- Many different languages are spoken throughout the world, making it more and more important to speak another language. With so many Hispanics now living in the United States, Spanish speakers are needed in almost every profession from fast food to medicine. The ability to speak Spanish will be a great asset to you as you live in this multicultural world.

- Did you know that there are approximately 14.5 million Spanish speakers living in the United States? You may be able to think of friends, neighbors, or people in your community who are native Spanish speakers. You might even see and hear Spanish every day, without realizing it. Directions, advertisements, and signs are often printed in both Spanish and English.

ACTIVITY 1 • HOW WILL LEARNING SPANISH HELP ME?

Think of all the Spanish words you have heard before. You might already know these words: *hola* (hello), *adiós* (goodbye), *sí* (yes), *no* (no), *amigo* (friend), *por favor* (please), *muchas gracias* (thanks a lot), and *de nada* (you're welcome). Do you realize that by knowing these words and a few more, you can carry on a conversation with a native Spanish speaker?

Performance Challenge

Individual 1 You just read a few reasons why you should learn Spanish. Now explain why you like learning Spanish and why you want to learn more. Share your ideas with a friend or a family member. Ask them why they would like to learn Spanish.

Performance Challenge

Individual 2 Make a list of at least five Spanish words that you already know. (Examples: *taco, rodeo, mosquito*)

Performance Challenge

Group Divide the class into teams. A student from each team will go to the chalkboard where several familiar Spanish words are written. The teacher will then call out a word in English and the first student to identify/point to the correct Spanish word on the board wins a point.

ACTIVITY 2 • WHERE IS SPANISH SPOKEN?   POWER-GLIDE SPANISH JUNIOR I

Where is Spanish Spoken?

ACTIVITY 2

✓ In this activity you will:
→ Learn about Spanish-speaking countries.

 Disc **1** Track **2**

Can you name two countries where Spanish is spoken?

1. *Spain*
2. *Mexico*

If you said *México* and Spain, *España*, you are correct. Mexico is a neighbor to the United States and Spain is where the Spanish language originated. As you may already know, Spanish is spoken in several countries throughout the world. It is most commonly spoken in Spain, Central America, and South America, but Spanish speakers can be found in practically every country in the world. Look at the map below and identify the countries where Spanish is the official language: Spain, Puerto Rico, Cuba, Dominican Republic, Mexico, Guatemala, Honduras, Belize, El Salvador, Nicaragua, Costa Rica, Panama, Cuba, Colombia, Venezuela, Ecuador, Peru, Bolivia, Chile, Paraguay, Argentina, Uruguay.

¿Sabías qué...?—Did you know...?
People who live in Puerto Rico are American citizens. Puerto Rico is not one of the fifty states, but it is called a "Free Associated State" and is part of the United States. Listen to the names of the Spanish-speaking countries on the map and try repeating them out loud.

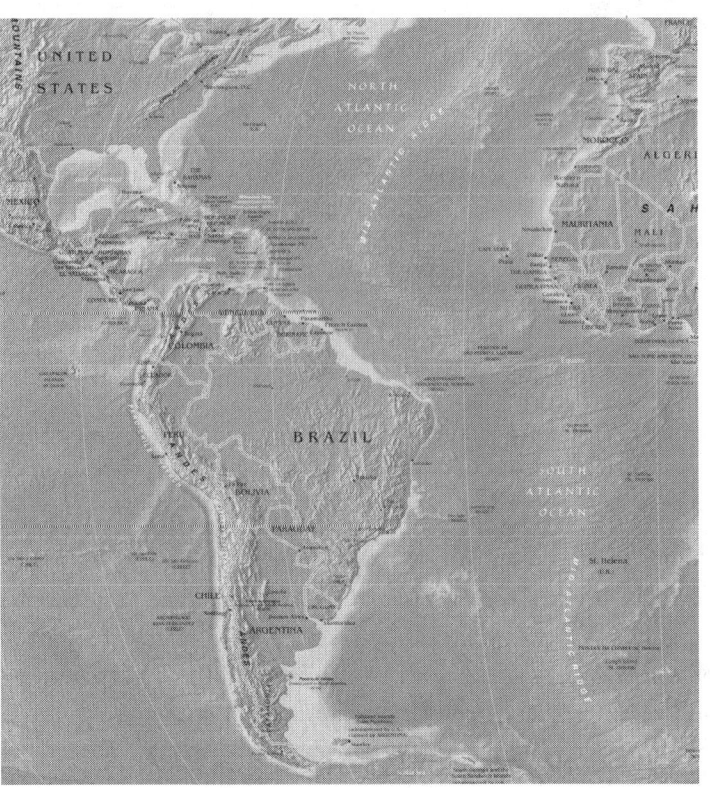

Las naciones

INSTRUCTIONS   Now that you can name many of the Spanish-speaking countries, try singing them in a song. Listen and sing along. When you're done, check the English translation in Appendix A, on page 252.

Las naciones (Sung to the tune of "The Eensy Weensy Spider")

Puerto Rico, Cuba,
España, México,
República Dominica,
Honduras y Belice,
Guatemala,
Nicaragua, Costa Rica,
Panamá, Colombia,
Venezuela.

Ecuador, El Salvador,
Bolivia, Perú,
Chile y Paraguay,
Y Uruguay también,
Argentina, y así
Recordamos a los países
Latinoamericanos.

Performance Challenge

Individual 1   Find out as much as you can about a Spanish-speaking country. Write down a few of the interesting things that you discover about it.

Performance Challenge

Individual 2   Practice singing "*Las naciones*" and perform it for your family and friends.

Common Greetings and Phrases

¡Hola! Hi! You probably already know a lot of Spanish words and greetings. Here are several phrases that are very important and useful when you are speaking Spanish.

INSTRUCTIONS Listen to and repeat the following words and phrases.

✓ **In this activity you will:**
→ Listen to and practice saying Spanish greetings and phrases.

 Disc 1 Track 3

Greetings and Phrases

English	Spanish
Hello.	Hola.
Good morning.	Buenos días.
How are you?	¿Cómo estás?
Fine, thanks.	Bien, gracias.
What is your name?	¿Cómo te llamas?
My name is ____.	Me llamo ____.
It's nice to meet you.	Mucho gusto.
Do you speak Spanish?	¿Hablas español?
Yes, I speak Spanish.	Sí, hablo español.
A little.	Un poco.
I don't understand.	No comprendo.
Goodbye.	Adiós.

Greetings Quiz

INSTRUCTIONS *Bueno.* See what you can do on your own. Identify the correct meaning of each word and phrase. Check your answers in Appendix A, on page 252.

1. *Adiós.* B
   A. A little.
   B. Goodbye.
   C. Hello.

2. *¿Cómo te llamas?* B
   A. How are you?
   B. What is your name?
   C. Do you speak Spanish?

3. *No comprendo.* A
   A. I don't understand.
   B. Fine, thanks.
   C. Good morning.

4. *Bien, gracias.* C
   A. Good morning.
   B. A little.
   C. Fine, thanks.

5. *Hola.* B
   A. Goodbye.
   B. Hello.
   C. How are you?

6. *Un poco.* C
   A. I don't understand.
   B. Good morning.
   C. A little.

ACTIVITY 3 • COMMON GREETINGS AND PHRASES

Performance Challenge

Individual   On several square pieces of paper, write out the Spanish greetings and phrases and their English translations. Place the squares face down. Pick up two squares at a time until you can pick up a matching set. (Example: *Hola.* Hello.)

Performance Challenge

Group   Have each student work with a partner and practice using common greetings and phrases. Students should switch partners and continue practicing with the same greetings and phrases. Make sure students alter the order of their phrases with each partner.

ACTIVITY 4 • ANIMAL VOCABULARY					POWER-GLIDE SPANISH JUNIOR I

Animal Vocabulary

ACTIVITY 4

 In this activity you will:
→ Learn to identify the Spanish names of animals.

 Disc **1**   Track **4**

INSTRUCTIONS   Here are a few animals that you should be familiar with. Listen to and repeat the Spanish names of these animals.

bear
el oso

tiger
el tigre

dog
el perro

lion
el león

cat
el gato

Now you are ready to learn about some new animals. Many animals that you know about are also common in Spanish-speaking countries. Listen to the names of these animals and repeat them out loud.

ACTIVITY 4 • ANIMAL VOCABULARY

Animal Story

INSTRUCTIONS You are going to read a story about animals using your new vocabulary. Make sure you refer back to your vocabulary list as you are reading. Listen first and then read the story out loud on your own.

There are *muchos animales* on the farm. *Hay las vacas, las ovejas, los cerdos, los caballos, los gatos, y los perros.* They all *viven* together. *Los caballos y las vacas son* the *grandes* on the farm. Every day *los caballos corren* very *rápidamente y las vacas comen mucho. El cerdo y la oveja* like to *dormir.* There is *un pájaro* on the farm *y el pájaro vuela* in the sky.

Hay also *muchos animales* in *el zoológico. Hay los elefantes, las serpientes, los tigres, los leones, y* more. I like *los tigres y los elefantes mucho. El león es mi favorito. El tigre y el león saltan* very well *y corren* very *rápidamente. Los elefantes no corren* very *rápidamente, pero* they *comen mucho.*

After you have listened to the story and read it out loud, go back and circle all the words you know in Spanish. You should have a good idea of the meaning of the story.

Translating Exercise

INSTRUCTIONS Look for the following words in the story and see if you can tell what they mean by reading the context of the sentence around them. Check your answers in Appendix A, on page 252.

Your Translations

Spanish Word	Translation
1. *hay*	
2. *grandes*	
3. *rápidamente*	
4. *mucho*	
5. *el zoológico*	
6. *favorito*	
7. *pero*	

ACTIVITY 4 • ANIMAL VOCABULARY

Performance Challenge

Individual   Choose your favorite animal from the vocabulary list. Draw your own picture of it below and describe why you like that animal. Use as much Spanish as you can.

My Favorite Animal

Why I Like It

....

....

....

....

....

....

Performance Challenge

Group   Create an action for each vocabulary word. As a word is called out, the students must act out the correct action as quickly as possible. If a student acts out the wrong action or is too slow, they have to sit down. The one student left standing at the end of the game wins.

What's in a Name?

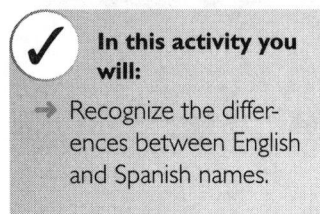

In this activity you will:
→ Recognize the differences between English and Spanish names.

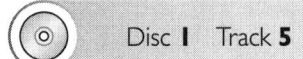

Disc **1** Track **5**

Many names in Spanish are similar to names in English, but not all English names have Spanish equivalents and not all Spanish names have English equivalents. Many names are spelled the same in both languages but are pronounced differently. Here is a short list of common Spanish names and their English equivalents. Do any of them look familiar to you?

INSTRUCTIONS Choose a name from the list to be your Spanish code name as you continue to learn more Spanish.

Girl's Names

English	Spanish
Alisha, Alice	Alicia
Anita	Anita
Anna	Ana
Barbara	Bárbara
Carmen	Carmen
Caroline	Carolina
Catherine, Kathryn	Catalina
Claudia	Claudia
Christina, Kristen	Cristina
Ellen	Elena
Lisa	Elisa
Lucy	Lucía
Margaret	Margarita
Mary	María
Martha	Marta

Girl's Names (cont.)

English	Spanish
Sarah	*Sara*
Theresa	*Teresa*

Boy's Names

English	Spanish
Alexander	*Alejandro*
Anthony	*Antonio (Toño)*
Carl	*Carlos*
Daniel	*Daniel*
Steven	*Esteban*
Phillip	*Felipe*
James	*Jaime*
George	*Jorge*
Joseph	*José (Pepe)*
Joshua	*Josué*
John	*Juan*
Michael	*Miguel*
Paul	*Pablo*
Peter	*Pedro*
Richard	*Ricardo*
Robert	*Roberto*
Thomas	*Tomás*

Performance Challenge

Individual Think about Spanish-speaking people that you know. What are their names? Is their name a Spanish-sounding name? Can you think of an English name that is similar?

··
··
··
··
··
··

> **Performance Challenge**
>
> *Group* Have students introduce themselves to each other in Spanish using their new Spanish names. Have students make name tags for themselves to help other students remember the name they will go by while in Spanish class.

ACTIVITY 6 • LOS ANIMALES

Los animales

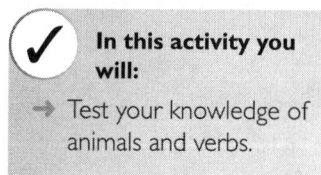

INSTRUCTIONS What are the animals doing? First listen to and then repeat the following sentences.

Animal Actions

English	Spanish/English
The pig eats corn.	El cerdo come el corn.
The cow lives in the stable.	La vaca vive en el establo.
The sheep jumps over the fence.	La oveja salta over the fence.
The dog sleeps in the garden.	El perro duerme en el jardín.
The elephant has big ears.	El elefante tiene big ears.
The horse runs very fast.	El caballo corre muy fast.
The bird flies above the trees.	El pájaro vuela above the trees.
The snake is green.	La serpiente es verde.

In this activity you will:
→ Test your knowledge of animals and verbs.

Disc 1   Track 6

Self Quiz

INSTRUCTIONS Now pick the correct verb from the list that makes the most sense in the sentence. Check your answers in Appendix A, on page 252.

1. *El cerdo* ____ **dirty.**
   A. *come*
   B. *es*
   C. *salta*

2. *La vaca* ____ **grass.**
   A. *vuela*
   B. *es*
   C. *come*

29

3. *El caballo* ____ en the pasture.
   A. *vive*
   B. *vuela*
   C. *tiene*

4. *El elefante* ____ a lot of food.
   A. *salta*
   B. *come*
   C. *es*

5. *La serpiente* ____ sneaky.
   A. *es*
   B. *salta*
   C. *come*

6. *El pájaro* ____ in the air.
   A. *duerme*
   B. *salta*
   C. *vuela*

7. *La gallina* ____ in the hen house.
   A. *vive*
   B. *corre*
   C. *tiene*

8. *El perro* ____ when he is happy.
   A. *es*
   B. *salta*
   C. *vuela*

Create Your Own Sentences

INSTRUCTIONS Guess what? Using what you've just learned, you can write your own sentences! Choose an animal from list A, a verb from list B, and add your own ending. You can use the verbs more than once but make sure you use them all.

Animals and Verbs

A	B
La gallina	*salta*
El elefante	*come*
La vaca	*es*
El pájaro	*vive*
La oveja	*vuela*
El cerdo	*corre*
El caballo	*duerme*
La serpiente	*tiene*
El perro	
El oso	
El león	
El gato	
El tigre	

1.
2.
3.
4.
5.
6.
7.
8.
9.
10.

Performance Challenge

Individual Imagine having one of the animals listed in this activity as a pet. Use all the Spanish you know including your new vocabulary words to explain why the animal you have chosen would be a good pet for you.

Performance Challenge

Group Assign small groups of students to represent a sports team, a business, a club, etc. Have the students in each group choose an animal to be their mascot, logo, etc. Have them describe in Spanish why that animal would best suit their organization.

ACTIVITY 7 • WHAT IS YOUR ANIMAL LIKE?

What is Your Animal Like?

ACTIVITY 7

Describing Animals

Animals come in many different sizes, shapes, colors, and have different personalities. You will learn how to describe animals in this activity.

Colors

INSTRUCTIONS Listen to the colors in Spanish and repeat them out loud. Then, color in the boxes with the correct color to help you remember them.

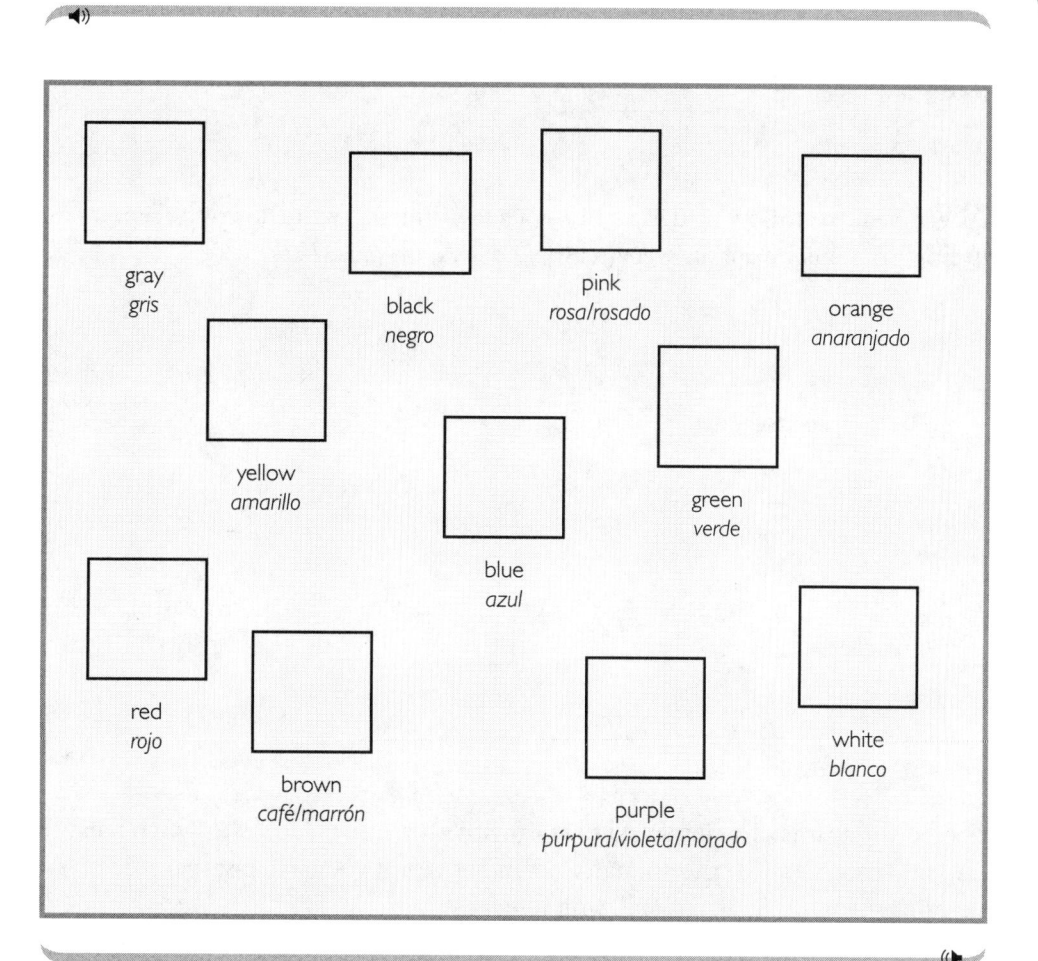

In this activity you will:
→ Learn how to use descriptive adjectives.

Disc **1** Track **7**

gray
gris

black
negro

pink
rosa/rosado

orange
anaranjado

yellow
amarillo

green
verde

blue
azul

red
rojo

brown
café/marrón

purple
púrpura/violeta/morado

white
blanco

33

Adjectives

Now you can say what color an animal is, but there are other words you can learn to describe an animal in more detail. Wouldn't you like to tell everyone about your tall, friendly elephant; your fierce, orange cat; and your loud, friendly cow?

INSTRUCTIONS Listen to and repeat these new adjectives and try to do your best impression of the word as you are saying it. For example, say *"alto"* and stretch your arms above your head to show how tall you are.

Animal Adjectives

English	Spanish
big	*grande*
small	*pequeño*
ferocious/fierce	*feroz*
noisy	*ruidoso*
nice	*amable*
fast	*rápido*
tall	*alto*
short	*bajo*

As you hear the following descriptions of a few animals, write down the sentences in English. Check your answers in Appendix A, on page 252.

1. *El león es grande y feroz.*

   ....

2. *La vaca es amable y negra.*

   ....

3. *Mi cerdo es ruidoso y rosado.*

   ....

4. *El caballo es alto y rápido.*

   ....

See how easy it is? You just need to start with an animal, add *"es,"* which means "is," and then describe the animal. Remember that if you have just two adjectives describing your animal, use *"y,"* which means "and."

Create Your Own Sentences

INSTRUCTIONS   Now it's your turn. Create sentences in Spanish with the following animals and adjectives. Check your answers in Appendix A, on page 252.

1. Hen—friendly and brown

   .... es .... y ....

2. Dog—brown and big

   .... es .... y ....

3. Bird—noisy and small

   .... es .... y ....

4. Tiger—orange and black

   .... es .... y ....

Draw and Describe

INSTRUCTIONS   Listen to the descriptions of three animals and draw a picture of each of them. Each description will be repeated three times. Check your answers in Appendix A, on page 253.

ex. *La vaca es grande, y blanca y negra.*
The sentence will be repeated three times, and then you will draw a big, brown cow in the draw box.

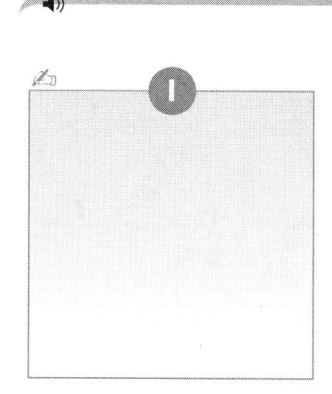

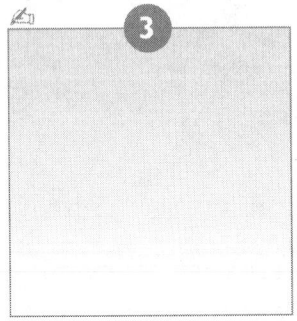

Performance Challenge

Individual Take a walk outside and look for as many animals as you can. Write down a detailed description of how each of these animals look.

....
....
....
....
....
....

Performance Challenge

Group Working in pairs students will draw and describe animals. One student will describe all the details of an animal while the other student draws it. Then, students will switch roles.

La gallinita roja: Part I

ACTIVITY 8

INSTRUCTIONS Listen to the following vocabulary words from the story of *La gallinita roja*.

Vocabulary

English	Spanish
once upon a time	*había una vez*
a little red hen	*una gallinita roja*
chickens	*gallinas*
she	*ella*
who	*quién*
plants	*plantas*
wheat	*el trigo*
one day	*un día*
asked	*pidió*
the rooster	*el gallo*
and	*y*
parts	*partes*
the duck	*el pato*
very well	*muy bien*
and so	*y así*
bread	*pan*
flour	*harina*

In this activity you will:
→ Understand the Spanish words and phrases in the story of "The Little Red Hen."

Disc **1** Track **8**

Vocabulary (cont.)

English	Spanish
all year	*todo el año*

The Little Red Hen—*La gallinita roja:* Part 1

INSTRUCTIONS First listen and follow along as the story is read to you. Then read the story out loud on your own to practice reading and speaking Spanish correctly. The English translation is in Appendix A, on page 253.

Había una vez, there was *una gallinita roja*. She lived in the barnyard with the other *gallinas* and roosters and ducks and geese. One day, this *gallinita roja* found a few grains of wheat. *Ella* decided that, instead of eating them, *ella* would plant them.

"*¿Quién* will help me *plantar* the wheat?" *ella* asked.

"Not I," *dijo* the rooster.

"Not I," *dijo* the duck.

"Not I," *dijo* the goose.

"Very well," *dijo la gallinita roja*. "I will do it myself."

And so *la gallinita roja* dug a little trench in the dirt with her beak and carefully planted each grain of wheat. *Ella* covered the seeds, *las semillas*, and stamped the dirt down just so. *Ella* gave them a little *agua* every day. Soon her *semillas* grew into little green sprouts. *Ella* kept watering them and made sure her sprouts got plenty of sunlight. Before long, they grew into fine, tall wheat *plantas*.

The *plantas* got heavy ears of *trigo* on them that gradually turned ripe and golden. The rest of the *plantas de trigo* dried and also turned a pale golden yellow. Finally, *un día, la gallinita roja* decided it was time to harvest her *trigo*.

"*¿Quién* will help me harvest *el trigo?*" *ella pidió*.

"Not I," *dijo el gallo*.

"Not I," *dijo* the duck.

"Not I," *dijo* the goose.

"Very well," *dijo la gallinita roja*, "I will do it myself."

Y así la gallinita roja cut down *su* fine, tall *plantas de trigo y* cut off the ripe heads of grain. Then it was time to thresh *el trigo*, to separate the good, edible *partes* from the hard, prickly *partes*.

"*¿Quién* will help me thresh *el trigo?*" *pidió la gallinita roja*.

"Not I," *dijo el gallo*.

"Not I," *dijo el pato*.

"Not I," *dijo* the goose.

"*Muy bien,*" *dijo la gallinita roja*. "I will do it myself."

Y así la gallinita roja threshed *su trigo* until *ella* had a little bag full of plump, golden grains of *trigo*. *La gallinita roja* decided *ella* wanted to make *pan* with it, so *ella* needed to take it to the mill to grind it into *harina*.

"*¿Quién* will help me grind *el trigo?*" *pidió la gallinita roja*.

"Not I," *dijo el gallo*.

"Not I," *dijo el pato*.

"Not I," *dijo la gansa*.

"*Muy bien,*" *dijo la gallinita roja*. "I will do it myself."

Y así la gallinita roja carried *su bolsa de trigo* to the mill, where *ella* ground it into *harina*. *Ella* brought *su bolsa de harina* back home. After waiting *todo el año*, it was finally time to make *pan*.

Comprehension Check

INSTRUCTIONS   Answer the following comprehension questions. Check your answers in Appendix A, on page 253.

1. What did *la gallinita roja* plant and then harvest?

   ....

2. Did any of the other farm animals help her?

   ....

3. What did *la gallinita roja* want to make with the *harina*?

   ....

Performance Challenge

Individual   Practice your Spanish pronunciation by telling the story of *La gallinita roja* to a friend or family member. Use as many Spanish words from the story as you can.

Performance Challenge

Group   In groups of four act out the story of *La gallinita roja*. Use the story segment in this activity as a script. Students will play the roles of the little red hen, the rooster, the duck, and the goose.

Animal Culture

Animals in Spanish-speaking Countries

There are many different animals in the world. Some animals can only live in certain areas and not in others. One special place is the Galápagos Islands in the Pacific Ocean. These islands are a part of Ecuador. About half of the species of animals that live on the islands cannot be found anywhere else in the world. The blue-footed booby is a very fascinating bird that is found in the Galápagos Islands.

Here is some interesting information about what you can find in several other Spanish-speaking areas of the world.

- In Puerto Rico you can find a small tree frog called a *coquí*. There are many varieties of *coquís*. They get their name from the special sound that they make "kokee kokee." Legend says that the *coquí* can only live in Puerto Rico and will quickly die if removed from its island home.
- Near Cuba you can swim with dolphins, turtles, whale sharks, moray eels, rays, and barracuda.
- Panama means "the place of abundant fish" and in Panama you will find an abundance of wildlife, fresh seafood, and many other things. It is the "country of abundance."
- Venezuela is home to a variety of exotic plants and animals including the jaguar, ocelot, tapir, armadillo, anteater, and the longest snake in the world, the anaconda.
- In Andalucia, España you will find mountain goats, deer, mongoose—or *meloncillo* in Spanish—and the royal owl.

Animals in Costa Rica

The *Parque Nacional Tortuguero* (National Park of Turtle Catchers) in Costa Rica is known for turtle nesting. During different times of the year along the Caribbean coast, green, hawksbill, loggerhead, and giant leather back turtles crawl up on the beach and deposit their eggs. You can also see crocodiles, freshwater turtles, manatees, tapirs, jaguars, anteaters, ocelots, and howler monkeys in this area. Are you wondering what some of these animals are like? Keep reading to learn more about each of them.

- A manatee is a large, gray mammal that lives in the water and has a paddle-shaped tail. An adult manatee will average about 9–10 feet long and will weigh about 800–1,200 pounds. Wow!

In this activity you will:
→ Read about animals living in Spanish-speaking countries.

ACTIVITY 9 • ANIMAL CULTURE

POWER-GLIDE SPANISH JUNIOR I

- The tapir is related to the primitive horse and rhinoceros. There are 4 species of the tapir and all of them are endangered. Baby tapirs weigh between 15–25 pounds at birth. Tapirs have four toes on their front feet and three toes on each back foot to help them walk in muddy and soft ground.
- The ocelot is from the large cat family. It swims well and is known for its distinct appearance. Ocelots have dark, brown irregular spots and stripes lined with black on a yellowish background. Ocelots weigh about twice that of a large domestic cat.
- The howler monkey is the loudest monkey and the loudest land animal. Its call can be heard up to three miles. Howler monkeys are the largest monkeys in North, South, and Central America. Males are black/brown and females are lighter in color. They can weigh 8–22 pounds and are 2–4 feet tall.

Compare and Contrast Exercise

Look at all of the animals you just read about. Which one do you think is the most unusual? Which animals do you think you would most like to see? Have you heard of any of these animals before? What is your favorite animal? Do you see any similarities between the new animals that you just read about and the animals that you already knew about? What foods do you think these new animals might eat? (Knowing where they live might help you with that answer.)

INSTRUCTIONS   Using these questions as a guide, write 2–3 paragraphs in English comparing and contrasting these new animals and the animals that you are already familiar with. You can also comment on your favorites, or what you find most interesting or unique about each animal.

....
....
....
....
....
....
....
....
....
....

Performance Challenge

Individual Take some time to look up more animals that are common in Spanish-speaking countries around the world. Find out more about a few of them. Using the Spanish that you know, describe these animals and where they live.

Performance Challenge

Group Give small groups of students pictures and information about one of the new animals they've learned about in this activity. Have each group study their animal and put together a poster with facts and pictures on it that they will present to the class.

SECTION 1.1.1 • ARRIVAL IN SPAIN

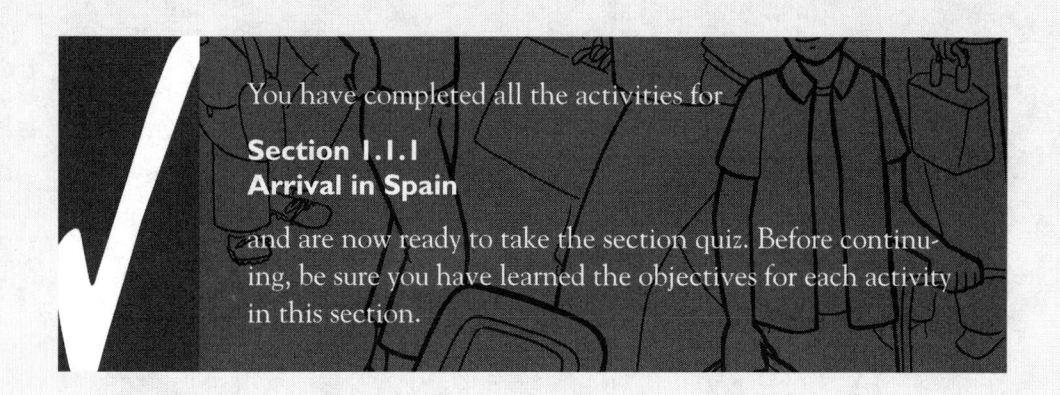

> You have completed all the activities for
>
> **Section 1.1.1**
> **Arrival in Spain**
>
> and are now ready to take the section quiz. Before continuing, be sure you have learned the objectives for each activity in this section.

Section 1.1.1 Quiz

INSTRUCTIONS Choose the correct word from the list below to fill in the blanks of the postcard. Don't try to use all of the words in the table, just pick the words that make the most sense in each sentence. Check your answers in Appendix A, on page 263.

ex. ¿Cómo __estás__?

Postcard Word Options

Spanish Words		
Hola	come	estás
inglés	te llamas	un poco
vuela	feroz	es
pequeño	mucho gusto	vive
Adiós	español	el león

¡Querido _____ (friend or family member)!

¡1._____! ¿Cómo 2._____? Estoy muy bien. I am learning mucho 3._____. Ahora mi animal favorito es 4._____. I learned that el león 5._____ muy grande y 6._____. También, el león 7._____ en the jungle. Pues, estoy 8._____ lonesome.

¡Adiós!

_____
(your Spanish name)

45

INSTRUCTIONS Draw a line connecting each of the animals to their correct names in Spanish.

9. la vaca

10. el tigre

11. el cerdo

12. el elefante

13. el caballo

14. el león

15. la oveja

16. el pájaro

INSTRUCTIONS Write out the meaning of the underlined word in the following sentences.

17. **The lion *es grande* y fierce.**

18. **El *perro vive* en the doghouse.**

19. *La vaca come* corn.

   ....

20. The elephant *es* tall *y gris*.

   ....

21. *La oveja salta* over the fence.

   ....

La Gallinita Roja Pollo

Legend of the Sword

"*¡Eso es!*" Tony shouts suddenly, holding up a take-out box from *La Gallinita Roja* restaurant. You open the box carefully. Inside, you find not leftover food, but a small book with a worn black leather cover. It's filled with Grandpa Glen's messy handwriting.

"It's his travel journal," *explica* Lisa. "He takes it on all his *viajes*." She turns to the last written *pagina* in the book. "The last entry was *ayer*, yesterday," she tells you, "but all it says is '*el rancho de cuarenta y cuatro hombres*' and 'the legend of the sword.'"

"Great, another obscure legend," Tony says. "How are we going to find out about this one?"

"*Pienso que* I can *ayudarles*," says *la inspectora*. She reaches into her briefcase and pulls out a scroll of parchment.

In this section you will:

- Improve your reading and listening comprehension skills with a very short story.
- Improve your translation skills by writing the English equivalents of several Spanish animal names and answering questions about different animals.
- Improve your Spanish vocabulary by matching animals with the Spanish adjectives that describe them.
- Improve your Spanish vocabulary by learning farm-related words.
- Learn a song about the animals that live on a farm.
- Learn about farms in other countries.
- Improve your Spanish vocabulary with nouns, verbs, pronouns, and conjunctions from a story.

(continued)

Disc 1 Track 9

SECTION 1.1.2 • LEGEND OF THE SWORD   POWER-GLIDE SPANISH JUNIOR I

✓ **In this section you will:**

→ Check your reading comprehension with questions based on a story.
→ Improve your grammar skills by learning about present tense verbs in Spanish.
→ Improve your writing skills by creating present-tense Spanish sentences of your own.
→ Improve your reading and listening comprehension skills with two very short stories.
→ Master new Spanish vocabulary with match-and-learn squares.
→ Improve your writing skills by describing what your farm would be like, using the farm- and animal-related vocabulary you have studied.
→ Learn to use the Spanish numbers from 1-20.
→ Learn a new song about numbers and dogs.
→ Learn about the music and dances of Spanish-speaking countries.

La Leyenda of the Sword de los Siete Knights

Había una vez a master weaponsmith. His *nombre* was *Alfonso Martinez de Gutierrez*. He poured all his skills into making one sword, *una espada muy especial*. It was sharp *como un* razor but *fuerte* enough to resist the mightiest blow. It was swift and bitter *como un* winter wind from *las montañas*. Alfonso thought that such an amazing *espada* could never know defeat, and he gave it to the king, *el rey*.

El rey gave Alfonso fine *regalos* in exchange for *la espada* and even made him a knight, *un caballero*. *El rey era un buen rey*, and he used *la espada* to defend his people. *Como* Alfonso thought, *la espada* always saw *el rey* through to *la victoria*. In time, though, *el rey* grew old and died, and his son, *su hijo*, took the throne.

El hijo no fue un buen rey. He used *la espada* to conquer and oppress. *El hijo de Alfonso* and *seis* other *caballeros* knew that *el rey* had to be stopped, but how? They waited for *una oportunidad*.

El rey decided to take his *caballeros* and invade a neighboring *reino*. The path led over tall *montañas*. It was narrow and dangerous, yes, *muy peligroso*. While *el rey y sus caballeros* were in *las montañas*, a terrible storm arose. Mighty *vientos* almost blew them off the narrow path. *Los relámpagos* flashed, and *los truenos* crashed deafeningly. The horse, *el caballo*, *del rey* panicked, *y el rey* fell off the narrow path to his doom. The magnificent *espada* was not destroyed, though. *Los caballeros* found it on a narrow ledge just below the path.

They *decidieron* that *la espada* had to be hidden away, so that it would not be misused again. They hid *la espada* in *una cueva* deep in *las montañas*. They set challenges and traps all along *la cueva* and built mighty gates of stone and steel to bar *la entrada* to *la cueva*. In the gate, they set *siete* locks, and each of them took one key, *una llave*. In case *la espada* were ever needed for good, they carved *un mapa* into a piece of stone near *la cueva*. They broke *el mapa* into *siete pedazos*, and each of them took *un pedazo* as well as *una llave*.

Los caballeros went their separate ways and never met again. *Sus hijos*, and in turn *los hijos de sus hijos*, guarded *las llaves y los pedazos del mapa*, but in time, the meaning slipped out of understanding, *los pedazos* were lost, *y la leyenda de la espada* was almost forgotten.

"There is *la leyenda* your *abuelo* mentioned," *la inspectora* tells you, "and *yo sé* where *el rancho de cuarenta y cuatro hombres* is. It's an old-fashioned estate, not far from here. I'll tell you about the rest of my case on the way."

You all pile into Inspector Gutierrez's *auto*, and as soon as *el auto* is out of the driveway, she begins. "*Nuestro rey* has a cousin named *Don Ramón de Traición*. *El rey y Don Traición* were *amigos* as children, *pero* they had a falling-out *cuando el rey* discovered that *Don Traición* and the laboratory he ran were dealing in illegal chemicals and selling *información* related to national *seguridad* to the highest bidder. The actions of *el rey* ruined *Don Traición*'s business and left him a ruined and desperate man. During this downfall, something must have snapped. He began claiming that he, *no el rey*, was rightful heir to *el trono*. He threatened that if *nuestro rey* did not give up the throne within *diez días*, millions would die. He also announced a reward for anyone who could lead him to the Knights' Sword, in hopes that it will make him invincible."

"Can he really hurt that many *personas?*" Lisa asks.

"*Desgraciadamente, sí*. He can," *la inspectora* Gutierrez replies grimly. "Before it was sold, his *laboratorio* put in orbit a satellite that collects solar energy. It can focus the energy it collects into a single, concentrated beam. Directed at a city, that beam could kill tens of thousands of *personas* in *segundos*. Your country's space program is trying to dismantle the satellite, but so far without luck. We must stop *Don Traición* here, or *muchas personas en todo el mundo* will be in danger."

"Does he have Grandpa Glen?" Tony asks.

"We don't know, *pero* we think so," *la inspectora* tells you. She stops her *auto* at the gate of *el rancho de los cuarenta y cuatro hombres*. "The ranch belongs to *descendientes* of one of *los caballeros*," she tells you. "Wait here while I get *permiso* for us to *entrar*."

La inspectora Gutierrez returns moments later with *un hombre* who opens the gate and ushers you inside. Once inside, you check Grandpa Glen's travel journal for more clues.

"*La llave número uno está* under *el trono del gallo*," you read aloud.

"*Llave número uno*—that means key number one!" *exclama* Tony.

"*Trono* means throne," you say, remembering *la leyenda de la espada*.

"And I'm pretty sure *gallo* means rooster," Lisa finishes. "Let's start looking for the rooster's throne."

Desgraciadamente, it looks like many years, *muchos años*, have passed since *el rancho* kept live *animales*. Finally, you spot *el trono del gallo*. A fancy weathervane, shaped like a crowing *gallo*, sits on a large metal base on top of the old barn. You get a ladder and climb up. You pry the weathervane off its base. Inside is a leather case cracked with age, and inside the case is a heavy bronze *llave* and a fist-sized piece of stone, *piedra*.

"Look at the case! It's *un mapa de España*," Tony comments. "And look! The city, *la ciudad,* of *Córdoba* has a star on it."

You climb down and show *la inspectora* what you have found. She *examina* the *pedazo* of stone. You notice that faint words are carved on the bottom of it. *La inspectora Gutierrez* translates aloud, "Born of *los gitanos,* in *el ritmo* of this dance beats *el corazón de España.*"

You're not sure what this clue means. You'll need to learn more about Spain to decipher it. To prepare for future challenges, now is also a good time to learn more Spanish vocabulary and to begin learning Spanish numbers.

ACTIVITY 10 • JOURNAL

Journal

ACTIVITY 10

El león y el tigre

INSTRUCTIONS   First listen to the story and follow along. Then read the story out loud and see what *el león y el tigre* are doing.

El león grande vive in the jungle and *come mucho* every *día*. *Un día el león* sees *el tigre y dice* (says), "*Tigre, ¿Cómo estás?*" *El tigre dice*, "*Muy bien, gracias. ¿Y tú?*" *El león dice*, "*Bien, gracias.*" *El león dice*, "*Adiós.*" *y el tigre dice*, "*¡Hasta mañana!*" *Entonces, el tigre come y el león corre* in the jungle. *El fin*.

Comprehension Check

INSTRUCTIONS   Answer the following comprehension questions. Check your answers in Appendix A, on page 253.

1. Where does the big lion live?

2. Who does the lion talk to?

3. How is the tiger doing?

4. When the tiger eats what does the lion do in the jungle?

Self Quiz

INSTRUCTIONS   *¡Bien hecho!* Now you are warmed up and ready to write down the English names of the following five animals. Check your answers in Appendix A, on page 253.

1. *el gato*

In this activity you will:

- Improve your reading and listening comprehension skills with a very short story.
- Improve your translation skills by writing the English equivalents of several Spanish animal names and answering questions about different animals.
- Improve your Spanish vocabulary by matching animals with the Spanish adjectives that describe them.

Disc 1   Track 10

53

2. *el caballo*

....

3. *la gallina*

....

4. *la vaca*

....

5. *el perro*

....

INSTRUCTIONS This time choose the correct translation of the following five sentences. First read each sentence out loud and then read the three possible translations of that sentence out loud. Circle the English translation that best matches the Spanish sentence.

6. **La vaca come corn.**
   A. The cat sleeps in the barn.
   B. The cow eats corn.
   C. The sheep jumps the fence.

7. **El ratón corre quickly.**
   A. The bird flies in the sky.
   B. The mouse runs quickly.
   C. The lion roars.

8. **El pájaro vuela in the sky.**
   A. The mouse runs fast.
   B. The horse eats in the pasture.
   C. The bird flies in the sky.

9. **El cerdo es smelly.**
   A. The pig is smelly.
   B. The hen lays eggs.
   C. The mouse runs fast.

10. **La oveja salta the fence.**
    A. The tiger has stripes.
    B. The bird flies in the sky.
    C. The sheep jumps the fence.

Refrán

Here is a *refrán* for you. Remember that a *refrán* is a Spanish saying. Practice saying this one out loud and try to remember it for future use.

¡No pierdas la cabeza!

Literal translation: Don't lose your head
Meaning: Take it easy!

ACTIVITY 10 • JOURNAL

INSTRUCTIONS It's your turn to describe the animals. Choose adjectives from the list that describe each of the animals below. Write one sentence for each animal using the adjectives you choose.

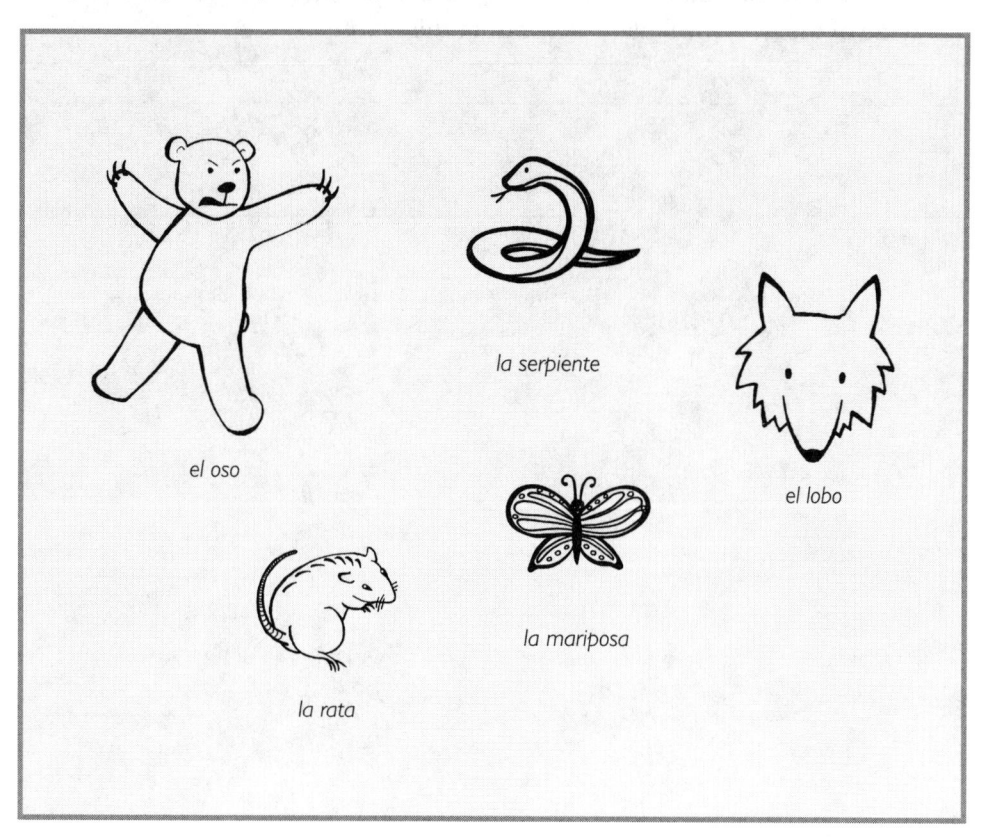

el oso

la serpiente

el lobo

la mariposa

la rata

Adjective Choices

Spanish		
amable	feroz	ruidoso
alto	grande	rápido
bajo	pequeño	

11. ....

12. ....

13. ....

14. ....

15. ....

ACTIVITY 10 • JOURNAL

Performance Challenge

Individual Draw a picture with at least five animals in it. Write a sentence below each animal describing what it is doing in the picture. Use some of the new vocabulary words from this activity.

1. ....

2. ....

3. ....

4. ....

5. ....

Performance Challenge

Group Play "Animal Bingo." Have students draw small pictures of each of the new animals on a grid-like game card. Call out the names of each animal or describe them in Spanish. The first student to mark off four animals in a row wins.

En la granja

You are going to visit a farm today. First, you will need to learn a few new Spanish words so that you can sing a song about the animals on the farm.

INSTRUCTIONS Listen to and learn the following words.

Farm Vocabulary

English	Spanish
the country	el campo
big farm	granja grande
dog	perro
to play	jugar
good friends	amigos buenos
cat	gato
very quick	muy veloz
mice	ratones
chickens/hens	gallinas

In this activity you will:
- Improve your Spanish vocabulary by learning farm-related words.
- Learn a song about the animals that live on a farm.

Disc 1 Track 11

Now listen to a song about a farm and the animals that live there. Sing along when you are ready. The English translation is in Appendix A, on page 254.

En la granja (Sung to the tune of "If You're Happy and You Know It")

En el campo, hay una granja grande.
En la granja, hay un perro amable,
Y el perro le gusta jugar
Con sus amigos buenos.
En la granja, hay un perro amable.

En el campo, hay una granja grande.
En la granja, hay un gato muy veloz,
Y el gato persigue a

Los ratones y gallinas.
En la granja, hay un gato muy veloz.

En el campo, hay una granja grande.
En la granja, hay un cerdo gordo, sí,
Y el cerdo come todo lo que
El granjero trae.
En la granja, hay un cerdo gordo, sí.

En el campo, hay una granja grande.
En la granja, hay una oveja, sí.
La oveja queda tranquilamente
Siempre en el prado.
En la granja, hay una oveja, sí.

En el campo, hay una granja grande.
En la granja, hay un caballo fuerte.
El caballo siempre ayuda al
Granjero con todo.
En la granja, hay un caballo fuerte.

En el campo, hay una granja grande.
En la granja, hay un granjero bueno.
El granjero cuida a todos
Animales de la granja.
En la granja, hay un granjero bueno.

Comprehension Check

INSTRUCTIONS Answer the following comprehension questions. Check your answers in Appendix A, on page 254.

1. Is *la granja* large or small?

   ....

2. What does *el perro* like to do?

   ....

3. Which animal helps *el granjero* with everything?

   ....

ACTIVITY 11 • EN LA GRANJA

Performance Challenge

Individual 1 Practice singing *"En la granja."* Memorize at least two stanzas of the song and perform them for your family or friends.

Performance Challenge

Individual 2 Create an additional stanza for *"En la granja."* Follow the pattern of the other stanzas but describe a different animal on the farm.

....

....

....

....

....

....

....

....

....

....

....

....

Performance Challenge

Group Divide the class into six groups. Give each group one stanza of *"En la granja"* to perform for the rest of the class using actions, pictures, sounds, etc.

Farms

ACTIVITY 12

In this activity you will:
- Learn about farms in other countries.
- Improve your Spanish vocabulary by learning more farm-related words.

Disc 1 Track 12

Farms in Spanish-speaking Countries

Did you know that farmers and ranchers all over the world raise cattle, sheep, pigs, and other animals? There are many ranches and farms in Spanish-speaking countries. Here is some information about a few of them.

- Argentina is well known for producing many agricultural products. Argentina has a huge cattle industry and supplies beef to most of the world. Argentina is also famous for its big steaks and good barbecues.

- Have you ever seen an olive grove? Olives are the most abundant crop in Andalucia, España. There are millions of olive trees there, which produce 1/3 of Spain's olive oil. Olives are harvested starting in late November and continuing through January. Harvesting is sometimes still done by traditional methods. A net or cloth is spread under an olive tree, which is then beaten vigorously with a stick. The olives fall from the tree and are gathered in the nets. Family-owned olive groves are often harvested by the whole family, which can be a fun event. After the olives are harvested from the trees, they are taken to a mill, mashed into pulp, and pressed and filtered to make olive oil. Modern machinery and stainless steel have replaced many of the donkey-driven presses. Some smaller, family-owned groves still use the traditional donkey-driven presses.

- Colombia, a country in South America, is famous for growing coffee trees. The coffee tree is unique because is can bear flowers and ripened fruit at the same time. Farmers harvest the berries off the tree, put them into bags, and load them onto donkeys to take to a factory. Each tree yields about one pound of coffee each year.

INSTRUCTIONS What do you think of when you think about a farm? Write down a few things.

ACTIVITY 12 • FARMS

Do you think all farms are alike?

What are your three favorite things about a farm?

There are many ways to say farm in Spanish. You have learned that *la granja* means farm or ranch. These are a few of the other ways to say farm.

- *La chacra*—used in many Spanish-speaking countries
- *La finca*—used in Colombia and Puerto Rico
- *La hacienda*—used in many Spanish-speaking countries
- *El rancho*—used in Mexico

Remember that more than one of these words can be used in the same country. In the United States, farm or ranch are often used to describe the same place.

Compare and Contrast

INSTRUCTIONS   Can you name a few things that are the same between the farms that you know of in the United States and the farms you just learned about?

What is the most interesting thing that you've learned about the farms in Spanish-speaking countries?

ACTIVITY 12 • FARMS POWER-GLIDE SPANISH JUNIOR 1

Match and Learn

INSTRUCTIONS   Listen to the words, repeat, and then draw a line connecting the words to their matching pictures. Check your answers in Appendix A, on page 254.

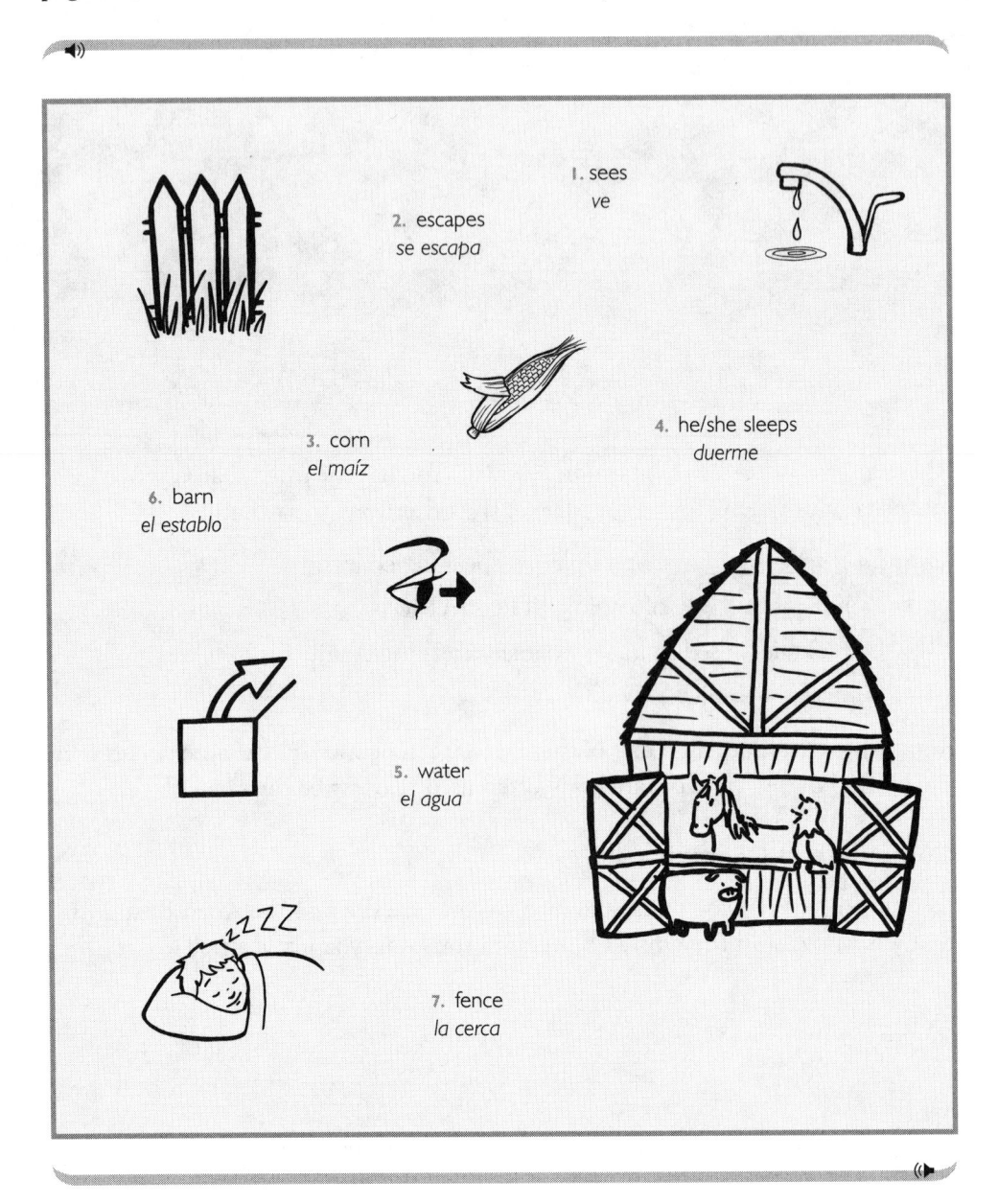

1. sees
   ve
2. escapes
   se escapa
3. corn
   el maíz
4. he/she sleeps
   duerme
5. water
   el agua
6. barn
   el establo
7. fence
   la cerca

Performance Challenge

Individual Create your own farm. Draw a farm below with at least ten items or animals in it and label them in Spanish. Show where the animals live, what they look like, or what they eat.

My Farm

Performance Challenge

Group Have small groups of students research one type of farm in a Spanish-speaking country. Each group will share what they learn with the rest of the class.

La gallinita roja: Part II

ACTIVITY 13 • LA GALLINITA ROJA: PART II

In this activity you will:
- Improve your Spanish vocabulary with nouns, verbs, pronouns, and conjunctions from a story.
- Check your reading comprehension with questions based on a story.

Disc 1 Track 13

INSTRUCTIONS Listen to the following vocabulary words from the story of *La gallinita roja*.

Vocabulary

English	Spanish
a little red hen	una gallinita roja
she	ella
who	quién
plant	plantar
said	dijo
wheat	el trigo
asked	pidió
the rooster	el gallo
and	y
the duck	el pato
very well	muy bien
and so	y así
bread	pan
prepare/make	preparar
the goose	la gansa
her bag	su bolsa
the oven	el horno
bake	cocer
a fire	un fuego

Vocabulary (cont.)

English	Spanish
the big	el grande
hot	caliente
loaf of bread	pan de molde
wonderful	maravilloso
to eat	comer
to plant	plantar
harvest	cosechar

The Little Red Hen—*La gallinita roja:* Part II

INSTRUCTIONS First listen and follow along as the story is read to you. Then read the story out loud on your own to practice reading and speaking Spanish correctly. The English translation is in Appendix A, on page 254.

"*¿Quién* will help me *preparar el pan?*" *pidió la gallinita roja.*

"Not I," *dijo el gallo.*

"Not I," *dijo el pato*.

"Not I," *dijo la gansa*.

"*Muy bien,*" *dijo la gallinita roja*. "I will do it myself."

Y *así ella* added y pounded y mixed y kneaded. Then *ella* let the *pan* dough rise. While it was rising, *ella* decided to heat up *el horno* to bake *el pan*.

"*¿Quién* will help me *cocer el pan?*" *pidió la gallinita roja*.

"Not I," *dijo el gallo*.

"Not I," *dijo el pato*.

"Not I," *dijo la gansa*.

"*Muy bien,*" *dijo la gallinita roja*. "I will do it myself."

Así ella lit *un fuego* in *el grande*, old-fashioned *horno* y carefully fed it and fanned it until *ella* had a nice, *caliente* bed of coals. Then *ella* put her *pan de molde* in *el horno* y let it *cocer*. Mm-mmm, it smelled *maravilloso!* Soon *el pan* was done y *la gallinita roja* took it out of *el horno*.

"Now," *dijo la gallinita roja*, "*quién* will help me *comer el pan?*"

"I will," *dijo el gallo*.

"I will," *dijo el pato*.

"I will," *dijo la gansa*.

"I don't think so," *dijo la gallinita roja*. "Did you help me *plantar el trigo?*"

"No," *dijo el gallo*.

"No," *dijo el pato*.

"No," *dijo la gansa*.

"Did you help me care for *el trigo?*" *pidió la gallinita roja*.

"No," *dijo el gallo*.

"No," *dijo el pato*.

"No," *dijo la gansa*.

"Did you help me *cosechar el trigo?*" *pidió la gallinita roja*.

"No," *dijo el gallo*.

"No," *dijo el pato*.

"No," *dijo la gansa*.

"Did you help me thresh *el trigo?*" *pidió la gallinita roja*.

"No," *dijo el gallo*.

"No," dijo el pato.

"No," dijo la gansa.

Comprehension Check

INSTRUCTIONS   Answer the following comprehension questions. Check your answers in Appendix A, on page 255.

1. Who helped *la gallinita roja* cook the bread?

   ....

2. Was the oven, *el horno,* big or small?

   ....

3. Who is willing to help *la gallinita roja* eat the bread?

   ....

Performance Challenge

Individual   Retell this part of the story of *"La gallinita roja"* to a friend or family member. Use as much Spanish as you can.

Performance Challenge

Group   Act out this segment of *"La gallinita roja"* in groups of four. Each student in the group will play the role of either the little red hen, the rooster, the duck, or the goose. Use the text as a script.

Present Tense

The present tense is used to describe things that are happening right now.

La vaca come el heno. The cow eats the hay.
(The cow eats the hay "now.")

El león corre rápidamente. The lion runs quickly.
(The lion runs quickly "now.")

INSTRUCTIONS Can you figure out what these sentences say in English? First read each sentence out loud and then write it down in English. Many times the meaning of a word is easier to figure out once you hear it. Check your answers in Appendix A, on page 255.

1. *El caballo vive* in the barn.

   ....

2. *El perro dice "guau, guau."*

   ....

3. *La gallina corre en la pastura.*

   ....

4. *La serpiente es* very *grande*.

   ....

5. *El cerdo come el maíz.*

   ....

Doing Things Now

When you look at the answers, see if you can put the word "now" into each sentence. The "now" will help you make sure that the sentence is in the present tense.

1. The horse lives in the barn "now."
   Sí, it works.
2. The dog says "woof, woof" "now."
   Sí, it works.
3. The chicken runs in the pasture "now."
   Sí, it works.

4. The snake is very big "now."
   Sí, it works.

5. The pig eats corn "now."
   Sí, it works.

Make Your Own Sentences

INSTRUCTIONS All of these verbs are in the present tense, so you just need to choose a subject, verb, and ending that go well together. You will be able to create many sentences with these choices.

Sentence Elements

Subjects	Present Tense Verbs	Endings
el caballo	come	feroz
la vaca	corre	alto
la granja	ve	pequeño
el perro	salta	mucho
el león	se escapa	grande
la gallina	es	amable
el pájaro	vuela	hermosa
el ratón	dice	ruidoso
el lobo	duerme	rápido

1. ....
2. ....
3. ....
4. ....
5. ....

Performance Challenge

Individual Using the subjects, verbs, and endings from this activity create as five correct Spanish sentences. Make sure each sentence makes sense in the present tense.

1. ....

ACTIVITY 14 • PRESENT TENSE   POWER-GLIDE SPANISH JUNIOR 1

2. ....
   ....
3. ....
   ....
4. ....
   ....
5. ....
   ....

Performance Challenge

Group On several pieces of paper write phrases from this activity like "*El caballo corre.*" Divide the class into two teams. One student from each team will look at the phrase and draw a picture on the chalkboard for their team. The team that guesses the correct phrase first wins a point.

La granja

ACTIVITY 15

INSTRUCTIONS Listen to the following story about a farm, then read it on your own. Figure out what all the animals are doing.

En la granja there are *muchos animales*. *Hay el caballo, la gallina, la vaca, el cerdo, el perro, el gato, la oveja,* y many more. They all *viven en el establo y comen en la pastura*. *La vaca* really likes *el maíz*. ¡*Y el cerdo come mucho* of everything! *El caballo y la oveja* eat in all *la pastura* every *día*. All of *los animales duermen en el establo*. *Los animales* are *muy amables y* I like them *mucho*.

Comprehension Check 1

INSTRUCTIONS Answer the following comprehension questions. Check your answers in Appendix A, on page 255.

1. Where are the animals?

2. Where do the animals eat?

3. What does the cow eat?

4. Where do all the animals sleep?

5. Are the animals friendly?

Match and Learn

INSTRUCTIONS Here are some more great words for *la granja*. Listen to and repeat these new words. Point to what you hear. Check your answers in Appendix A, on page 255.

In this activity you will:
- Improve your reading and listening comprehension skills with two very short stories.
- Master new Spanish vocabulary with match-and-learn squares.

Disc 1   Track 14

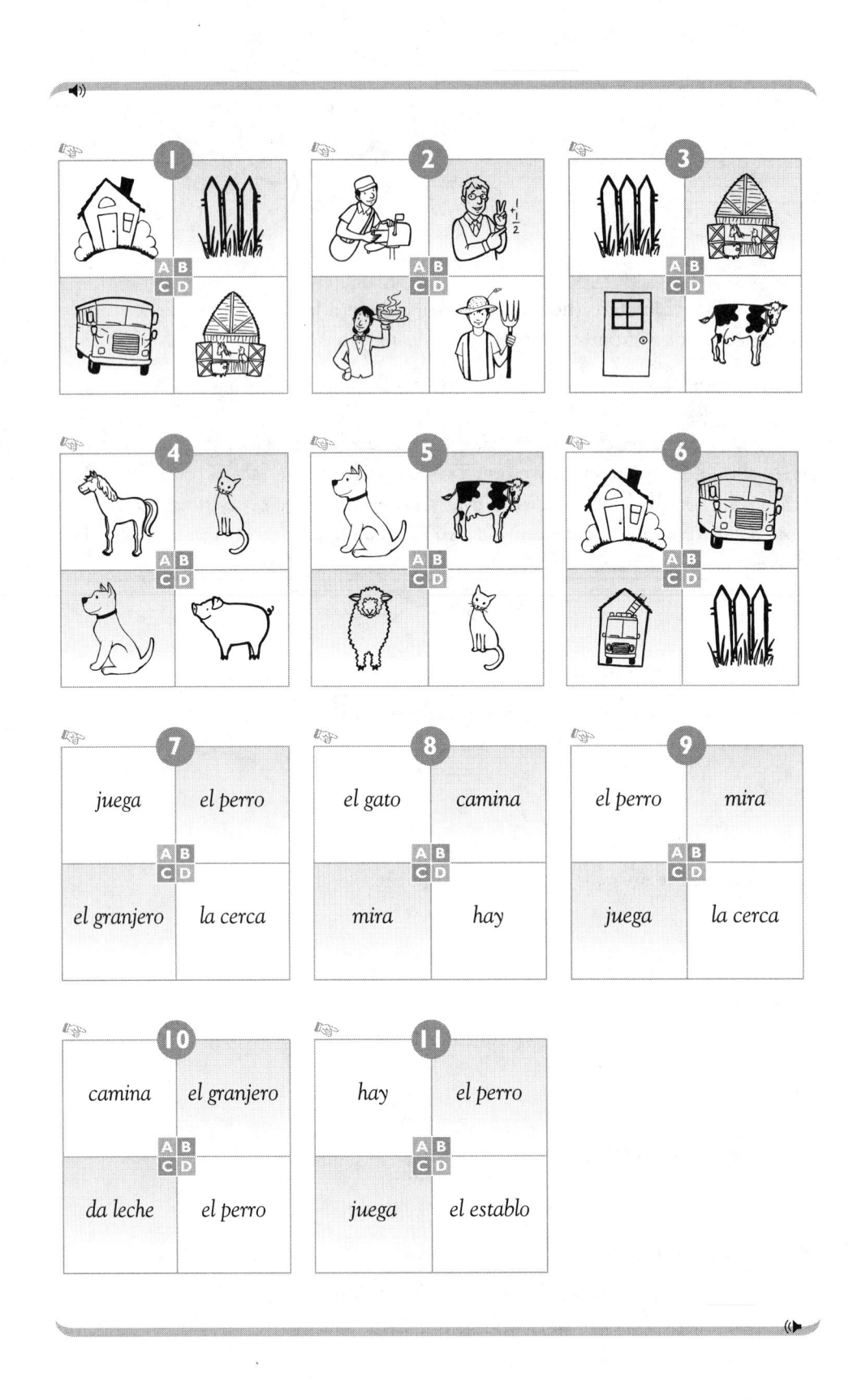

ACTIVITY 15 • LA GRANJA   POWER-GLIDE SPANISH JUNIOR 1

7
juega	el perro
el granjero	la cerca

8
el gato	camina
mira	hay

9
el perro	mira
juega	la cerca

10
camina	el granjero
da leche	el perro

11
hay	el perro
juega	el establo

A Friend's Farm

INSTRUCTIONS   Listen to the following story about a farm and then read it out loud on your own.

Aquí is *la granja* of *un amigo*. He *es un granjero*. *El granjero* has *muchos animales* y his favorite *es el caballo*. *El caballo se llama* "Spunky." Spunky *vive en la pastura* and *hay una cerca grande*. Spunky *come mucho heno* and *mucho maíz en el establo*. Spunky *es grande* and *café*. Spunky *es muy rápido*. Spunky *juega* with *la vaca y el cerdo* every *día*. *El granjero mira a los animales mucho y camina* to *el establo* to feed them.

Comprehension Check 2

INSTRUCTIONS   Answer the following comprehension questions. Check your answers in Appendix A, on page 255.

1. Who has the farm?

2. What animal is the farmer's favorite?

3. Where does Spunky eat hay and corn?

4. Spunky is big and what color?

5. What does the farmer watch?

Performance Challenge

Individual   Write and illustrate a short story about one of the animals on the farm. Describe what the animal you chose looks like and what it does on the farm. Use present tense verbs.

My Short Story

Performance Challenge

Group Divide the class into several small groups. Give each group a picture of a farm that they can describe using some of the new vocabulary from this activity.

What Would Your Farm Be Like?

ACTIVITY 16

In this activity you will:

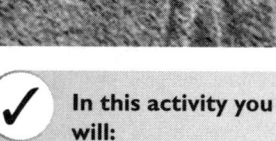

→ Improve your writing skills by describing what your farm would be like, using the farm- and animal-related vocabulary you have studied.

INSTRUCTIONS Imagine that you have your own farm. Write a short story, of at least two paragraphs, describing your farm. What animals do you have? What do they eat? Where do they live? What do they look like? Use your new vocabulary and as many Spanish words as you can. Fill in the rest with English. *¡Buena suerte!* (Good luck!) Feel free to add pictures to help you describe your farm. Have fun!

Performance Challenge

Individual Visit a local farm and learn more about how it works. Identify the Spanish names of the animals and items on the farm that you have learned. Add any important details you learn about at the farm you visit to your story.

Performance Challenge

Group Have students work in pairs and share their farm stories and illustrations with each other. Each pair of students should make a list comparing and contrasting their farm stories and illustrations. There should be many similarities but also some differences.

Numbers and Animals

ACTIVITY 17

Counting to 10

INSTRUCTIONS Do you remember how to count to 10? Try counting from 1 to 10 in Spanish.

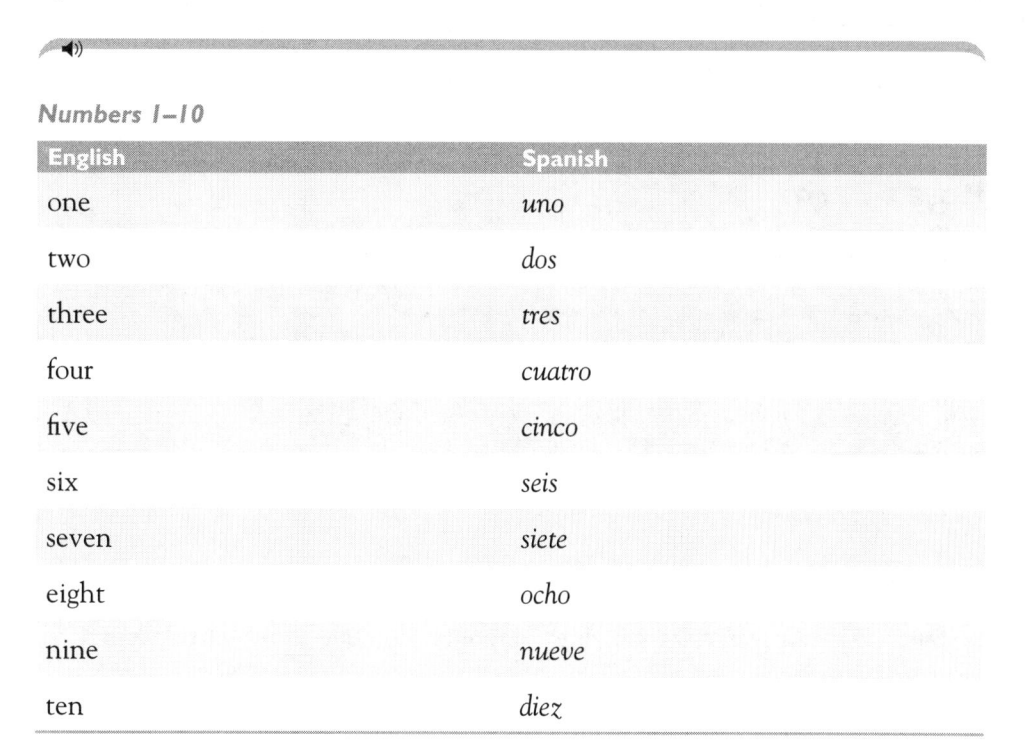

Numbers 1–10

English	Spanish
one	*uno*
two	*dos*
three	*tres*
four	*cuatro*
five	*cinco*
six	*seis*
seven	*siete*
eight	*ocho*
nine	*nueve*
ten	*diez*

In this activity you will:
- Learn to use the Spanish numbers from 1–20.
- Learn a new song about numbers and dogs.

Disc **1** Track **15**

Diez perritos

INSTRUCTIONS Now, sing a song about *perritos*—puppies—using numbers 1 through 10 in Spanish. The English translation is in Appendix A, on page 256.

Diez perritos (Sung to the tune of "Ten Little Indians")

Uno, dos, tres perritos,
Cuatro, cinco, seis perritos,
Siete, ocho, nueve perritos,
Diez perritos juegan.

Diez, nueve, ocho perritos,
Siete, seis, cinco perritos,
Cuatro, tres, dos perritos,
Un perrito juega.

Rosa's Farm

INSTRUCTIONS Listen, then read out loud on your own.

Rosa has *un elefante, dos perros, tres cerdos, cuatro ovejas, cinco gallinas, seis vacas, siete serpientes, ocho pájaros, nueve gatos, y diez caballos en su granja. ¡Los caballos are sus favoritos!*

Comprehension Check

INSTRUCTIONS Answer the following comprehension questions. Check your answers in Appendix A, on page 256.

1. How many horses does Rosa have?

   ....

2. How many hens does Rosa have?

   ....

3. Rosa has seven snakes and how many birds?

   ....

Counting to 20

Rosa would like to have a lot of animals on her farm some day and she needs to be able to count them. Can you count to 20?

INSTRUCTIONS Listen to and repeat numbers 11–20.

Numbers 11–20

English	Spanish
eleven	once
twelve	doce
thirteen	trece
fourteen	catorce
fifteen	quince
sixteen	dieciséis
seventeen	diecisiete
eighteen	dieciocho
nineteen	diecinueve
twenty	veinte

Now listen to and repeat the following numbers and animals.

Counting Animals

English	Spanish
twenty sheep	veinte ovejas
twelve hens	doce gallinas
eighteen pigs	dieciocho cerdos
fifteen horses	quince caballos
sixteen cows	dieciséis vacas
fourteen dogs	catorce perros

ACTIVITY 17 • NUMBERS AND ANIMALS

Match and Learn

INSTRUCTIONS Now listen and point to the number you hear. Check your answers in Appendix A, on page 256.

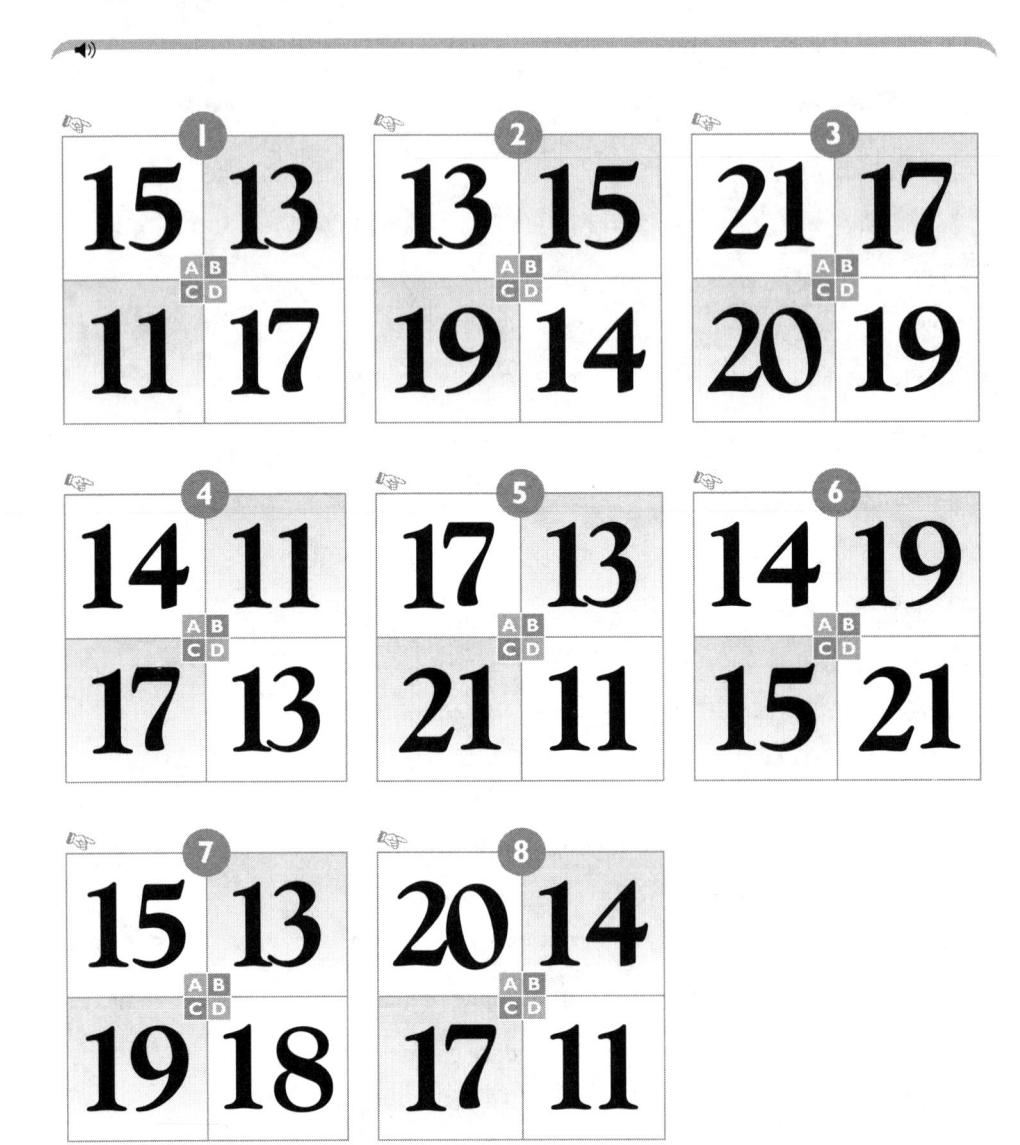

1.
A	B
15	13
11	17

2.
A	B
13	15
19	14

3.
A	B
21	17
20	19

4.
A	B
14	11
17	13

5.
A	B
17	13
21	11

6.
A	B
14	19
15	21

7.
A	B
15	13
19	18

8.
A	B
20	14
17	11

Performance Challenge

Individual Create your own song below using the animal words and numbers you have learned. Set your lyrics to an appropriate tune and practice singing it. Perform your song for your family and friends.

Performance Challenge

Group Give each student several cards with 1–20 of a specific animal on each card. Allow students to barter and trade animals in order to get close to a certain number, like 40. Example: "I'll give you *cuatro ovejas* for *catorce cerdos*." The student who is closest to the target number wins.

Cultural Music

In this activity you will:

→ Learn about the music and dances of Spanish-speaking countries.

Music is such an important part of life all over the world. Most cultures have a special style of music that they associate with and many cultures have songs that are very meaningful to them. As you learn more about music and listen to examples from all over the world, you will hear that all styles are unique and yet much the same. Music is often used to express moods, opinions, feelings, stories, history, etc. When you ask people what their favorite kind of music is, they will usually tell you that it depends on what they are doing or what kind of mood they are in. Thank goodness we have many styles of music to choose from.

It is impossible to use a specific name like "Latin American," "South American," or "Mexican" to really cover all Spanish music. There are many countries in Central and South America and within each country there are different styles of music that are common. You might find that the south end of one country and the north end of another country have more music in common that the two ends of the same country. The reason is that music comes from so many things: culture, experiences, families, friends, landscape, major events, and more. So you can see that people who live close together in similar conditions may have common tastes in music. It would be unfair to group all styles of music that are common and popular in a certain area under one title.

Take a look at some of the different styles of music, traditional dances, and some of the musical instruments that are common in Spanish-speaking countries. If you have access to the Internet, go to <http://www.power-glide.com/go/?key=spanish-music> for links to pictures, music, and dance instructions.

Dances

Flamenco

Flamenco dancing originated in southern Spain many years ago and is still very popular. Three elements make up *flamenco* dancing: singing, guitar playing, and dancing. The guitar and the dancer follow the singer while following the *compás*—a set rhythm that is unique to *flamenco*. Clapping and beating on a drum help the dancers and singers keep the beat. The guitar used is a special *flamenco* guitar that is similar to a classical guitar. A pick is usually used but sometimes a *flamenco* guitar player grows a really long thumbnail to produce the correct sound. There are songs with a light mood and some that are very heavy and sad sounding. *Flamenco* singing is unique. It is rough and guttural, sung deep in the throat. *Flamenco* dancing is spirited and filled with tradition.

Mexican Hat Dance

Have you ever heard of the Mexican Hat Dance? You have probably heard the music before. The Mexican Hat Dance was originally created as a form of unity in *México* during the revolution and is considered a courting dance. Many important Mexican dance moves are used to create this dance. The familiar music that accompanies the Mexican Hat Dance is called *jarabe*, which is a combination of popular local songs. *Jarabes* are popular throughout *México* and have been especially popular symbols of dance and music in Central and Southern *México*.

While dancing, the women usually wear a *China Poblana*, a female servant outfit from the early 1800s. Each beautiful *China Poblana* is covered with sequins and embroidery. The men usually wear the *charro* suit which became popular with *mariachi* music in the early 1900s. The *charro* suit is a jacket and tight pants with silver buttons.

Dance Practice

INSTRUCTIONS Find a partner that would like to try the Mexican Hat Dance with you. Hopefully someone in your class or your family will be willing to give it a shot.

In this dance, partners face each other and hold hands. Jump and tap each heel alternately forward three times starting with the right foot. Here are the directions broken down into six steps:

1. Jump and tap right heel in front
2. Jump and tap left heel in front
3. Jump and tap right heel in front
4. Clap twice

Repeat these first four steps seven times.

5. Hook right elbows with partner and swing partner in a circle with eight small running steps
6. Reverse and swing your partner the other way

Repeat from the beginning.

Instruments

Castanets

Castanets are two pieces of wood held in one hand and are often referred to as "clappers" or "finger cymbals" because the fingers make the castanets clap together. The name comes from the Spanish word for chestnut, *castaña*, since castanets were originally made from that wood. Now they are also made from various woods, nutshells, ivory, plastic, and metal. Castanets are used to make the rhythmic, drum-like sounds in many forms of Spanish music and they are especially popular in *flamenco* music. Dancers often play the castanets while they are dancing. They play the basic beat with one castanet and the dance rhythm with the castanet in the other hand. It takes a lot of practice to be able to dance and play the castanets. Castanets are found in most Spanish music and they are also used in Central and South American music. You can buy a cheap set of castanets that have been made by a machine in music stores everywhere. They work but don't have the same beautiful sound as a handmade pair of castanets. Making castanets by hand is a dying art, there are very few castanet makers left in Spain.

Charango

The *charango* is an instrument with strings similar to a guitar. The *charango* is used on the Canary Islands and in Central and South America. In *Perú*, the *charango* might be called a mandolin.

Maracas

You probably know what a *maraca* is and you might have used one. *Maracas* are "shakers" that are generally used when playing music. *Maracas* were originally made from gourds that were hollowed out and filled with seeds. *Maracas* are used in playing music and they are also used to make noise with at a party.

Music Assignment

Now that you have learned about a few styles of Spanish music and about a few instruments, what do you think? Do you think you have ever listened to music from a Spanish-speaking country before? Your assignment is to find some Spanish music and listen to it. There are many ways to find Spanish music. Ask at your local library to see if they have any music from Spanish-speaking countries that you could check out, listen to a radio station from a Spanish-speaking country on the internet, or buy/borrow a Spanish tape, record, or CD to listen to. Enjoy yourself!

Maracas

It might be fun to make your own *maracas*. Here's a list of some things you will need to make them.
- Paper plates
- Dried beans, popcorn, or rice
- Stapler
- Crayons, markers, or paint
- Streamers, decorations

You can make a *maraca* by putting beans, rice, or popcorn on one plate and placing the other plate over the top. Staple two plates together. (Make sure that you have the tops of each place facing each other so the popcorn has room to bounce around in there.) Or you can make a one plate *maraca*. Fold the plate in half, add the popcorn, and then staple the rims together. It will look like half a circle.

Now decorate with crayons, markers, or paint. You might want to add other decorations or streamers. Be creative and enjoy shaking your *maracas* to the music!

Performance Challenge

Individual   Find out more about one of the traditional dances or common instruments introduced in this activity. Write down a few things you learn. Perform the dance, or make and play the instrument you choose for your friends and family members.

ACTIVITY 18 • CULTURAL MUSIC

....
....
....
....
....
....

Performance Challenge

Group Practice the Mexican Hat Dance with the music and perform it for another class or for the rest of the school. A few students could play the maracas and the castanets while the other students dance.

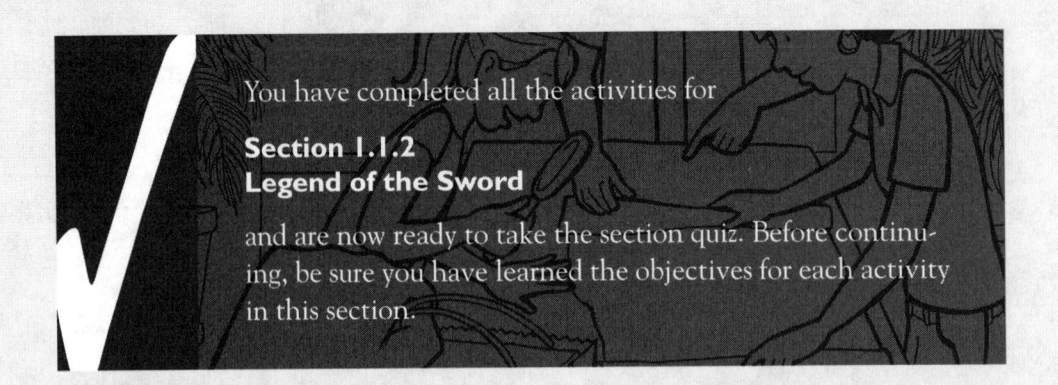

SECTION 1.1.2 • LEGEND OF THE SWORD

POWER-GLIDE SPANISH JUNIOR 1

You have completed all the activities for

Section 1.1.2
Legend of the Sword

and are now ready to take the section quiz. Before continuing, be sure you have learned the objectives for each activity in this section.

Section 1.1.2 Quiz

INSTRUCTIONS Write the Spanish name of the animal on the line beneath it and draw a line connecting the animal picture with an appropriate adjective in the box. Check your answers in Appendix A, on page 264.

ruidoso

amable

1. _____

2. _____

grande

pequeño

feroz

3. _____

rápido

alto

4. _____

5. _____

SECTION 1.1.2 • LEGEND OF THE SWORD

INSTRUCTIONS Read each of the following sentences out loud and then draw a picture to match each sentence. Have fun!

11. *La vaca come el maíz.*

12. *El perro es* very *ruidoso.*

13. *El cerdo dice* "oink, oink."

14. *El caballo vive en el establo.*

15. *La oveja mira* at *el granjero.*

INSTRUCTIONS Write a few sentences about animals. Use the words from the list to help you build sentences.

ex. *El pájaro vuelo alto en el cielo.*

Sentence Elements

Animals	Verbs	Adjectives	Places
la vaca	come	ruidoso (a)	en el establo
el perro	corre	grande	en la pastura
la oveja	vive	amable	en la granja
el gato	salta	feroz	en el cielo
la gallina	dice	alto (a)	en la casa
la serpiente	ve	bajo (a)	en el jardín

Sentence Elements *(cont.)*

Animals	Verbs	Adjectives	Places
el pájaro	vuela	pequeño (a)	en el árbol
el caballo	duerme	rápido (a)	en la chacra
el cerdo	es	bonito (a)	en la finca

✓ You have completed all the sections for
Module 1.1
Before continuing, be sure you have learned the objectives for each activity in this module.

Bay of
Biscay
Bordeaux
Bilbao
Porto
PYRENEES
Zaragoza
ANDORRA
Madrid
Tagus
Lisbon
SPAIN
Valencia
Balearic
Sea
Sevilla
Gibraltar
(U.K.)
Málaga
Strait of Gibraltar
Ceuta
(SPAIN)
Alborán
Sea
Oran
Melilla
(SPAIN)
Rabat
Casablanca

Module 1.2

Keep these tips in mind as you progress through this module:
1. Read instructions carefully.
2. Repeat aloud all the Spanish words you hear on the audio CDs.
3. Learn at your own pace.
4. Have fun with the activities and practice your new language skills with others.
5. Record yourself speaking Spanish on tape so you can evaluate your own speaking progress.

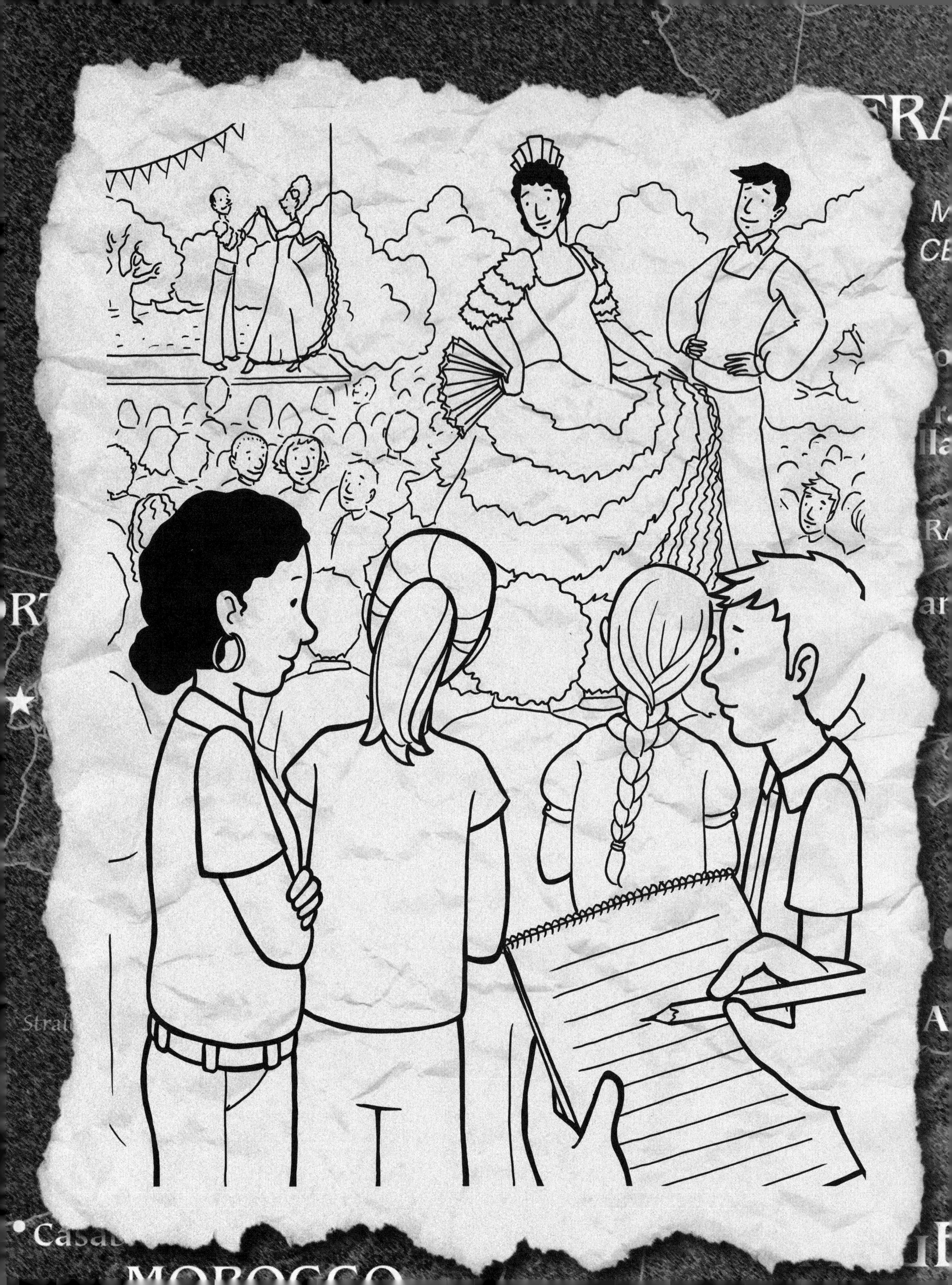
MOROCCO

A Flamenco Festival

While *la inspectora* drives, Tony, Lisa, *y tú* puzzle over the clue on your way to *la ciudad de Córdoba*. "Let's figure out *las partes en español* first," you suggest. "I think *los gitanos* means 'the gypsies.'"

"*El ritmo* sounds like 'the rhythm,'" Tony points out.

"And *el corazón de España* means 'the heart of Spain,'" Lisa finishes.

La inspectora turns on *el radio* in her *auto*, and *el auto* fills with *música—música de guitarra*, to be precise, with a definite *ritmo* to it. "*¿Qué* is this?" Lisa asks.

"It's *música folklórica*," *la inspectora* Gutierrez answers. "*Esta música* is often used in flamenco dancing… Hold on, flamenco dancing! That's it!"

"I think you're right!" you reply. "But what does flamenco dancing have to do with *la ciudad de Córdoba*?"

"*Pienso que* there's a flamenco festival there tonight," *la inspectora* Gutierrez tells you. "There will be dancers from all over *el mundo*. It will be a grand show, and maybe, *quizás*, it will give us our next clue."

The journey to *Córdoba* passes quickly, and soon you are all joining the crowds around the main dance pavilion, watching one couple swirl and tap their heels in perfect accompaniment to the live *guitarra* music. You watch them, fascinated, but Tony pulls out a notebook and starts scribbling.

"What are you doing?" you ask.

"It's Morse code!" Tony whispers excitedly. "Listen to their heels. They're tapping out Morse code. I'm writing down the message."

After *un momento*, Tony shows you what he's written. "The key lies beneath the shadow at seven," you read aloud.

"The estate of the second *caballero* isn't far from here," *dice la inspectora* Gutierrez, "and it's well-known for the huge sundial in its courtyard."

"We'll have to be there *a las siete* tomorrow morning," Lisa says.

In this section you will:

- Practice your writing skills and review what you've learned about animals and farms.
- Read and listen to a short passage, then answer questions on it.
- Improve your Spanish vocabulary by learning about different workplaces and jobs.
- Improve your Spanish conversational skills and vocabulary by learning how to describe different occupations in Spanish.
- Improve your Spanish conversation skills and vocabulary by studying a short passage on the library, then learning phrases that help you interact politely with Spanish-speaking people.
- Learn about employment situations in Spanish-speaking countries.

(continued)

Disc 2 Track 1

In this section you will:

- Improve your Spanish vocabulary and storytelling skills with the third part of the story of the Little Red Hen.
- Solidify your mastery of work-related vocabulary.
- Learn to build correct questions and statements in Spanish.
- Improve your Spanish listening comprehension and reading skills with a short passage and related questions.
- Use the Spanish vocabulary and grammar skills you have acquired so far to write your own short story.

After a pleasant dinner of *tortilla española* and *flan*, *ustedes* get some rest. Early the next *mañana*, *la inspectora* takes you to the estate of the second *caballero*. You have no *dificultad* spotting the sundial, but you might have some *dificultad* reaching it. The gates don't open to *el público* until ten. Lisa *y tú*, being the smallest, climb the wall around the estate and hurry to the sundial. You check your watch. It's seven o'clock. *Son las siete*. You reach the sundial and look closely at its elaborate mosaic. Next to *el número siete* is an emerald green tile that doesn't fit the rest of the pattern. You pry it loose. In the hollow beneath it is another *llave*, with its handle shaped like a graceful flamenco dancer, and another *pedazo* of *el mapa*.

Lisa *y tú* hurry back to the others, and *la inspectora* reads the clue carved into this *pedazo*. "*Cuando* staying long in this pond of *pensamientos*, even ducklings can turn into swans."

To decipher this clue, you'll need to learn about work and education. It wouldn't hurt to hone your storytelling abilities either.

… ACTIVITY 19 • JOURNAL

Journal

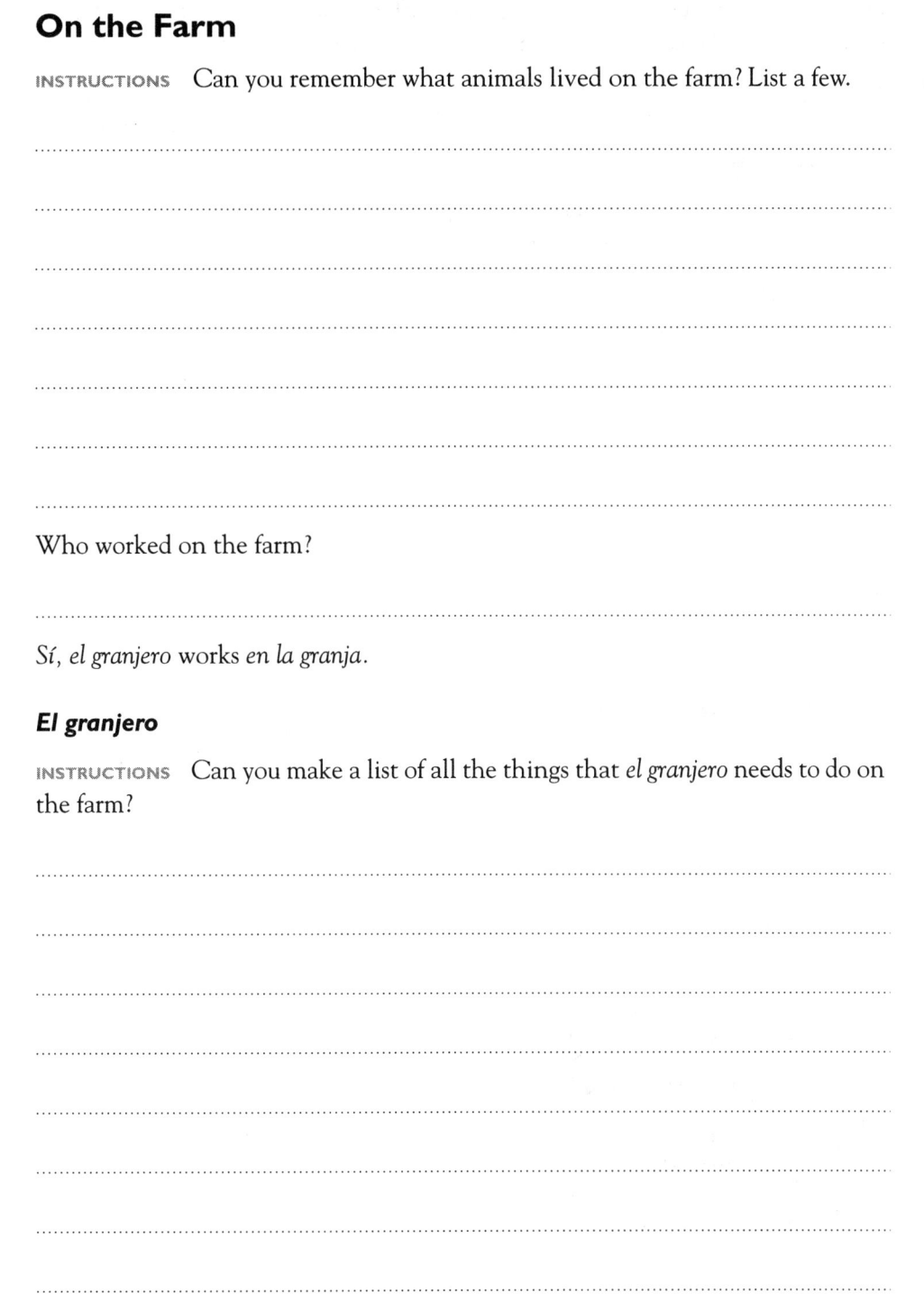

ACTIVITY 19

On the Farm

INSTRUCTIONS Can you remember what animals lived on the farm? List a few.

....

....

....

....

....

Who worked on the farm?

....

Sí, el granjero works *en la granja.*

El granjero

INSTRUCTIONS Can you make a list of all the things that *el granjero* needs to do on the farm?

....

....

....

....

....

....

In this activity you will:

→ Practice your writing skills and review what you've learned about animals and farms.
→ Read and listen to a short passage, then answer questions on it.

Disc **2** Track **2**

Chores

INSTRUCTIONS Listen to and read the following list of chores *un granjero* does *en la granja*. The English translation is in Appendix A, on page 256.

El granjero gives *el heno* y *el maíz* to *los animales todos los días. El granjero mira los animales* y cleans *el establo* y mows *la pastura. El granjero es muy ocupado. El granjero trabaja todos los días. Por la noche, el granjero duerme en la casa.*

Comprehension Check

INSTRUCTIONS Answer the following comprehension questions. Check your answers in Appendix A, on page 256.

1. What does the farmer feed the animals?

2. The farmer watches the animals and what does he clean?

3. Is the farmer busy?

4. How often does the farmer work?

Describe a Farm

INSTRUCTIONS Look at this farm picture and write down five sentences that describe it.

Refrán
Here's another *refrán*. Practice saying it out loud several times and try to use it today in a conversation.

No cantes gloria antes de victoria.
Literal translation: Don't sing glory before the victory.
Meaning: Don't count your chickens before they're hatched.

1. ....
2. ....
3. ....
4. ....
5. ....

Performance Challenge

Individual Make a list of all the things that *un granjero* needs to do on a farm. You should be able to think of at least five things *un granjero* does. Use the vocabulary you've just learned to help you out.

1. ....
2. ....
3. ....
4. ....
5. ....

Performance Challenge

Group Hold a farmer career day. Have small groups of students tell a little bit about one student in their group who will be a farmer for a day. They should describe some of the things their farmer does on the farm, what he or she likes to do/doesn't like to do, etc.

ACTIVITY 20 • JOBS POWER-GLIDE SPANISH JUNIOR I

Jobs

ACTIVITY 20

✓ **In this activity you will:**
→ Improve your Spanish vocabulary by learning about different workplaces and jobs.

◉ Disc **2** Track **3**

Workplaces

Everywhere you go someone is working. When you go to the *supermercado* (supermarket), someone is selling groceries. When you go to *la biblioteca* (library), someone is checking out books. When you go to *la panadería* (bakery), someone is making bread and cookies. When you go to *el banco* (bank), someone helps you with your money.

INSTRUCTIONS Listen to some common places that people work.

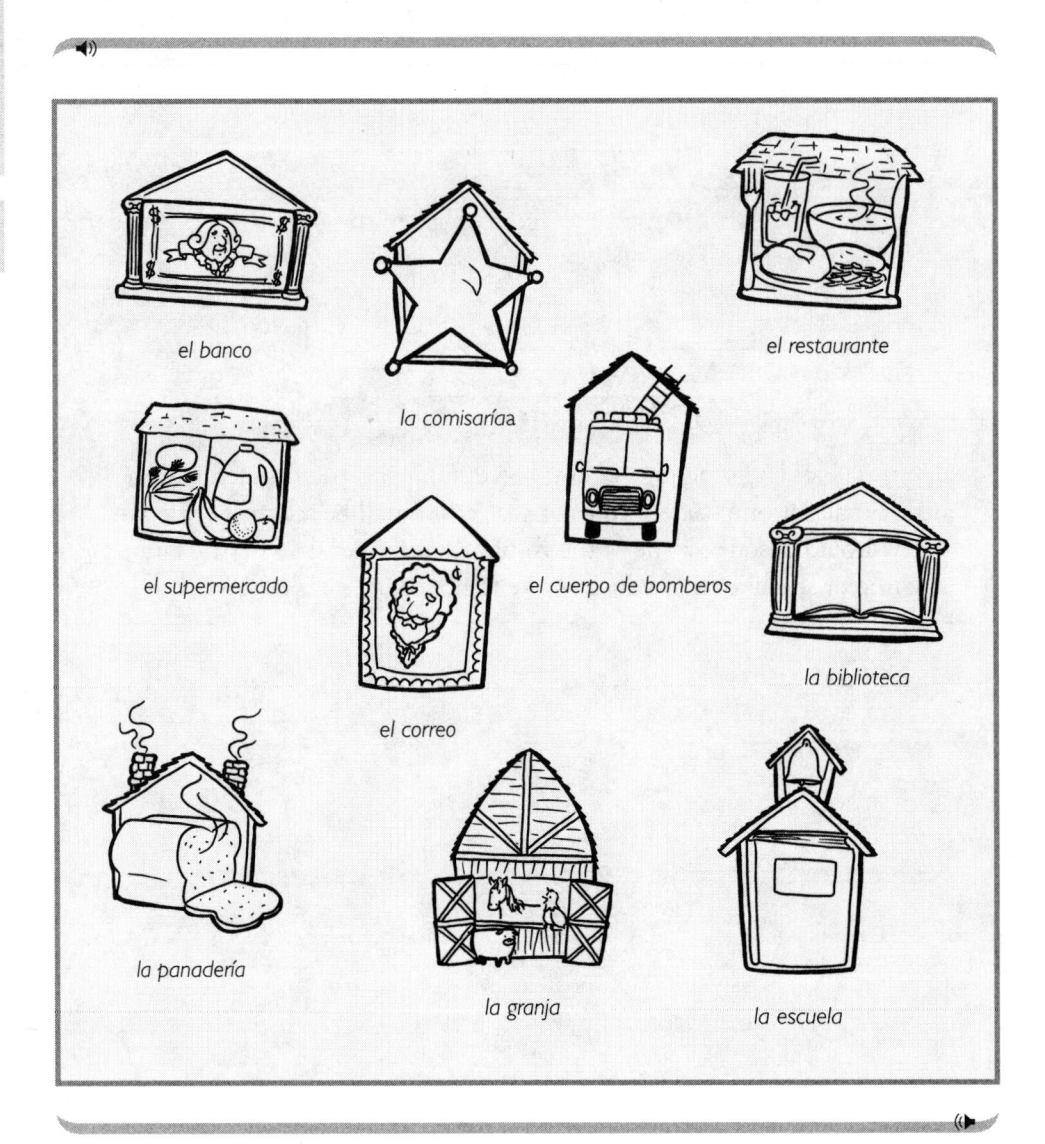

el banco

la comisaríaa

el restaurante

el supermercado

el cuerpo de bomberos

la biblioteca

el correo

la panadería

la granja

la escuela

ACTIVITY 20 • JOBS

Remembering Workplaces

Take a closer look at these new Spanish words. If you can find something in a word to use as a clue, then the word will be easier to remember. Look at these examples:

- *El supermercado*—Can you see the word "super" and something that looks like "market?"
- *El banco*—Can you see "banc" or "bank" in the word?
- *El correo*—Remember that *"corre"* means "to run." Think about the mail being "run" from house to house.
- *La panadería*—Do you see the word "pan?" Imagine a pan full of breads, cakes, and cookies.
- *El restaurante*—Looks almost exactly like "restaurant."
- *El cuerpo de bomberos*—Use the "bomb" in *"bomberos"* to remind you of fire.

There isn't a hint for all of these words, but when trying to learn new words it always helps to think of a clue. Be sure to try this the next time you need to learn something new.

Workers

INSTRUCTIONS Now you will meet the people who work at the places you just learned about.

- el cartero
- el granjero
- el tendero
- el panadero
- el maestro
- el camarero
- la banquera
- el policía
- la bibliotecaria
- el bombero

Little Shops

In Spanish-speaking countries there are many little shops or stands that have special names. They usually end with "-ería." These little stands sell specialty items. For example, one stand might sell just fruit. That stand would be called *"la frutería."* Another stand would sell only milk/dairy products and would be called *"la lechería."* A stand that only sells paper would be called *"la papelería."* Many times these specialty stands are found along the sidewalks and streets. Isn't it fun to learn all about other countries?

Listen to the following sentences explaining where each of these people work.

1. *El tendero* (grocer) works in *el supermercado*.
2. *El banquero* (banker) works in *el banco*.
3. *El cartero* (mail person) works in *el correo*.
4. *El bibliotecario* (librarian) works in *la biblioteca*.
5. *El panadero* (baker) works in *la panadería*.
6. *El policía* (police officer) works in *la comisaría*.
7. *El camarero* (waiter) works in *el restaurante*.
8. *El bombero* (fire fighter) works in *el cuerpo de bomberos*.
9. *El granjero* (farmer) works on *la granja*.
10. *El maestro* (teacher) works in *la escuela*.

Many of the words for these workers are similar to the names of the places they work. This will make it easier for you to remember them.

Translation Matching

INSTRUCTIONS   After listening to and reading the sentences above, match the Spanish words below with their appropriate English translations. Check your answers in Appendix A, on page 256.

1. **el supermercado**
    A. restaurant
    B. bakery
    C. supermarket

2. **el banco**
    A. post office
    B. bank
    C. farm

3. **el correo**
    A. supermarket
    B. post office
    C. bakery

4. *la biblioteca*
   A. library
   B. restaurant
   C. post office

5. *la panadería*
   A. bank
   B. school
   C. bakery

6. *la comisaría*
   A. school
   B. police station
   C. library

7. *el restaurante*
   A. post office
   B. fire station
   C. restaurant

8. *la escuela*
   A. school
   B. bakery
   C. bank

- Which job would you like the best?

  ....

- Which job do you think is the most work?

  ....

Performance Challenge

Individual 1   Do some research on your own to find out about some of the little shops and stands that are found in the marketplaces in Spanish-speaking countries. What kinds of things are sold in these little shops? Who works at them?

....

....

ACTIVITY 20 • JOBS

Performance Challenge

Individual 2 Choose one of the jobs you would like to have from the list. Write about why you think that job sounds interesting and fun. Use as many new Spanish words as you can.

Performance Challenge

Group Divide into several teams. Have a student from each team at the chalkboard. The teacher calls out a workplace or a worker in English and the students write out the Spanish translation. The first student to write the correct word gains a point for their team.

Trabajos

ACTIVITY 21

In this activity you will:
- Improve your Spanish conversational skills and vocabulary by learning how to describe different occupations in Spanish.

Disc **2** Track **4**

INSTRUCTIONS Listen to the following sentences and then read them out loud.

1. *El panadero trabaja en la panadería. El panadero trabaja* many *horas* each *día. El panadero cocina* all of *la comida.*
2. *El policía trabaja en la comisaría. El policía protege* the people. *El policía es muy* brave.
3. *El maestro trabaja en la escuela. El maestro enseña* the students.
4. *El cartero trabaja en el correo. El cartero trae* the mail to *las casas. El cartero camina mucho.*

Understanding

What do you think the word *trabaja* means? Can you figure it out?

El maestro trabaja en la escuela. El maestro is the teacher and *la escuela* is the school. What do you think the teacher is doing at the school? What is the policeman doing at the police station?

Did you guess "working?" *Sí, exactamente.*

They are "working." *Trabaja* means "works."

INSTRUCTIONS Read the same sentences again now that you know *trabaja* means "to work."

1. *El panadero trabaja en la panadería. El panadero trabaja* many *horas* each *día. El panadero cocina* (cooks) all of *la comida.*
2. *El policía trabaja en la comisaría. El policía protege* (protects) the people. *El policía es muy* brave.
3. *El maestro trabaja en la escuela. El maestro enseña* (teaches) the students.
4. *El cartero trabaja en el correo. El cartero trae* (brings) the mail to *las casas. El cartero camina mucho.*

At Work

INSTRUCTIONS When you are working, there are many important things to do. Listen to what some of those things are.

Work Actions

English	Spanish
listens	*escucha*
watches	*mira*
talks	*habla*
writes	*escribe*
works	*trabaja*

"Catch" the Meaning

INSTRUCTIONS Using the words that you know and the new vocabulary, try to "catch" the meaning of the following sentences. Read them out loud and then work on the meanings. Check your answers in Appendix A, on page 256.

En la oficina el jefe habla mucho y el secretario escribe mucho.

1. Where are they?

2. Who is *"el secretario?"*

El panadero mira el pan en the oven.

3. What is *"pan?"*

El maestro trabaja en su cuarto de clase.

4. What is *"el cuarto de clase?"*

El granjero escucha la radio en el establo.

5. What is the farmer doing?

Performance Challenge

Individual Use as much Spanish as you can to write "Help Wanted" ads for at least three of the jobs you have just learned about. Write out a basic job description and some requirements for people who want to apply for each job.

Performance Challenge

Group Divide the class into small teams. The teacher will describe a specific worker in Spanish. The team who correctly identifies the Spanish word for the worker described wins a point.

Other Words on the Job

In this activity you will:
- Improve your Spanish conversation skills and vocabulary by studying a short passage on the library, then learning phrases that help you interact politely with Spanish-speaking people.

Disc **2**   Track **5**

INSTRUCTIONS Listen to the following paragraph. Try to figure out what is being described.

Hay muchas personas aquí hoy. Todos leen los libros y las revistas. Es muy tranquilo en la biblioteca. Carlos viene al escritorio, "Perdón. ¿Puede Ud. decirme dónde están los periódicos?" "Por supuesto," dice el bibliotecario. "Los periódicos están cerca de la mesa y enfrente de la ventana." "Gracias," dice Carlos. "De nada," dice el bibliotecario. "Shh. Shh. Silencio por favor," dice el bibliotecario.

Can you tell what is being described?
Sí, la biblioteca.

Palabras nuevas

INSTRUCTIONS Listen to and repeat these new words from the library.

Words Used in the Library

English	Spanish
people	*las personas*
book	*el libro*
magazine	*la revista*
peaceful	*tranquilo*
pardon/excuse me	*perdón*
Where is...?	*¿Dónde está...?*
newspaper	*el periódico*
thank you	*gracias*

Words Used in the Library (cont.)

English	Spanish
you're welcome	de nada
table	la mesa
window	la ventana

La biblioteca

INSTRUCTIONS Read the paragraph about *la biblioteca* out loud with the audio, then answer the following questions.

Hay muchas personas aquí hoy. Todos leen los libros y las revistas. Es muy tranquilo en la biblioteca. Carlos viene al escritorio, "Perdón. ¿Puede Ud. decirme dónde están los periódicos?" "Por supuesto," dice el bibliotecario. "Los periódicos están cerca de la mesa y enfrente de la ventana." "Gracias," dice Carlos. "De nada," dice el bibliotecario. "Shh. Shh. Silencio por favor," dice el bibliotecario.

Comprehension Check

INSTRUCTIONS Answer the following comprehension questions. Check your answers in Appendix A, on page 256.

1. Are there many people in the library?

   ....

2. What are the people doing?

   ....

3. Is it very noisy and busy in the library?

   ....

4. What is Carlos looking for?

   ....

5. What do you think *"silencio"* means?

   ....

On the Job

When you are "on the job" you need to be polite and do a good job. It is very important that you know how to ask people to do things and how to help them. Here are some really helpful Spanish phrases.

INSTRUCTIONS Listen to and repeat the following words and phrases.

Words and Phrases

English	Spanish
Welcome.	Bienvenidos.
Can I help you?	¿Puedo ayudarle?
One moment please.	Un momento por favor.
Sit down please.	Siéntense por favor.
Slower please.	Más despacio por favor.
Thank you.	Gracias.
You're welcome.	De nada.

La clase

INSTRUCTIONS Here's a short paragraph in a *cuarto de clase* (classroom). Listen to it, read it out loud, then define the terms listed below. Check your answers in Appendix A, on page 256.

"*Bienvenidos a la clase hoy. Siéntense, por favor,*" *dice el maestro. Los estudiantes se sientan en la clase. Un estudiante nuevo trabaja mucho* but looks confused. *El maestro dice,* "*¿Puedo ayudarle?*" "*Sí, gracias,*" *dice el estudiante nuevo.* "*Esta clase es muy difícil* but very *interesante.*" *El maestro habla mucho y el estudiante nuevo dice,* "*Más despacio, por favor. Yo no entiendo* (understand)." *El maestro repite la información y* everything makes sense to *el estudiante.* "*Gracias,*" *dice el estudiante.*

There are several new words in this paragraph but many of them look like words you already know in English. See if you can figure out what they mean. Remember that these words are used in a classroom.

1. *estudiantes*

2. *difícil*

   ....

3. *interesante*

   ....

4. *repite*

   ....

5. *información*

   ....

It's fun when you can find Spanish words that look like English words. This can help you understand what you are reading.

> **Performance Challenge**
>
> **Individual** Go to a library, a restaurant, or another workplace and observe the people working there. Write down a few sentences describing the things the workers say and do.

....

....

....

....

....

....

....

> **Performance Challenge**
>
> **Group** Set up stations around the classroom where the students can "work at" and "visit" a few workplaces. Students should be assigned to ask for and do certain things so that they can use the new vocabulary words from this activity.

Job Culture

ACTIVITY 23

In this activity you will:
- Learn about employment situations in Spanish-speaking countries.

Many students in Spanish-speaking countries need to work to pay for their education and other expenses. Some students can work for their parents if they own a business. Working in *el supermercado* is also a very common job. Students are able to work 4–6 hours a day and still find time to go to school and to do their homework. It is often tough for students to find a job that allows them to continue going to school.

The fishing industry is very big in countries that have a coastal border. Many times, entire towns are supported by the fishing industry. Fishing boats and fishing jobs are often passed on from generation to generation in these towns. If you didn't like fishing, it could be a challenge to live in a fishing town because there may not be any other jobs available for you.

In some Spanish-speaking countries, workers have been given more rights and are able to run their own businesses now. Some factories, hotels, *supermercados*, and other businesses are being run by the workers. Workers are encouraged by this change in power and they feel that it will lead to increased wages and better working conditions. It is exciting to see positive change!

There are many of the same kinds of jobs in different countries and there are also some jobs that are unique to certain areas. Different languages sometimes describe the same job using different words. The Spanish word *bombero* comes from *bomba* which means "to pump." That gives you an idea of someone who pumps water to put out a fire.

Performance Challenge

Individual Research jobs in one of the Spanish-speaking countries. Make a list of some of the main industries and popular jobs that you learn about from your research.

ACTIVITY 23 • JOB CULTURE

Performance Challenge

Group Have students brainstorm about what kinds of jobs some students have while going to school here in the U.S. Also have students make a list of any family businesses they are familiar with.

La gallinita roja: Part III

In this activity you will:
- Improve your Spanish vocabulary and storytelling skills with the third part of the story of the Little Red Hen.

Disc **2**   Track **6**

INSTRUCTIONS Listen to the following vocabulary words from the story of *La gallinita roja*.

Vocabulary

English	Spanish
a little red hen	una gallinita roja
she	ella
to plant	plantar
said	dijo
wheat	el trigo
asked	pidió
the rooster	el gallo
the duck	el pato
the bread	el pan
prepare/make	preparar
the goose (feminine)	la gansa
her bag	su bolsa
the oven	el horno
bake	cocer
to eat	comer
other animals	otros animales
harvest	cosechar
heads	cabezas
but	pero

Vocabulary (cont.)

English	Spanish
share	compartir
all	todos
delicious	delicioso
the following/next day	el día siguiente
the dirt/earth	la tierra
together	juntos

The Little Red Hen—*La gallinita roja:* Part III

INSTRUCTIONS   First listen and follow along as the story is read to you. Then read the story out loud on your own to practice reading and speaking Spanish correctly. The English translation is in Appendix A, on page 256.

"Did you help me grind *el trigo?*" pidió la gallinita roja.

"No," dijo el gallo.

"No," dijo el pato.

"No," *dijo la gansa.*

"Did you help me *preparar el pan?*" *pidió la gallinita roja.*

"No," *dijo el gallo.*

"No," *dijo el pato.*

"No," *dijo la gansa.*

"Did you help me *cocer el pan?*" *pidió la gallinita roja.*

"No," *dijo el gallo.*

"No," *dijo el pato.*

"No," *dijo la gansa.*

"Well then," *dijo la gallinita roja,* "you didn't help me *plantar el trigo.* You didn't help me care for *el trigo.* You didn't help me *cosechar el trigo.* You didn't help me thresh *el trigo.* You didn't help me grind *el trigo.* You didn't help me *preparar el pan,* y you didn't help me *cocer el pan.* Do you think you have any right to *comer el pan?*"

The *otros animales* hung their *cabezas* in shame.

"No," *dijo el gallo.*

"No," *dijo el pato.*

"No," *dijo la gansa.*

"That's right," *dijo la gallinita roja,* "you don't. *Pero* just this once, I'll be nice y *compartir.*"

Y así todos los animales ate the fresh, *delicioso pan juntos. El día siguiente, la gansa* found some more grains of *trigo* lying in *la tierra.*

"Hey, look what I found!" *ella* called.

Todos los animales came over y helped her collect *el trigo,* y then *todos* of them planted the *trigo juntos.*

Comprehension Check

INSTRUCTIONS   Answer the following comprehension questions. Check your answers in Appendix A, on page 257.

1. Did the rooster, duck, and goose help *la gallinita roja* do anything?

   ....

2. Did *la gallinita roja* eat the delicious bread she made by herself?

   ....

3. What did the animals do together in the end of the story?

....

> **Performance Challenge**
>
> *Individual* Use the list of vocabulary words for *La gallinita roja* to write a short story of your own. Read your story to a family member or a friend. Use as many vocabulary words as you can.

....
....
....
....
....
....
....
....
....
....
....
....
....
....
....

> **Performance Challenge**
>
> *Group* In groups of four, create an alternate ending to the story of *La gallinita roja*. Perform the new ending for the rest of the class.

ACTIVITY 25 • EL TRABAJO: MATCHING

El trabajo: Matching

In this activity you will:
- Solidify your mastery of work-related vocabulary.
- Learn to build correct questions and statements in Spanish.

Disc **2**   Track **7**

INSTRUCTIONS   Listen to and learn the following words that might be used by people while they are at work.

Vocabulary

English	Spanish
people	*personas*
book	*el libro*
magazine	*la revista*
peaceful	*tranquilo*
comes	*viene*
pardon/excuse me	*perdón*
Where is…?	*¿Dónde está…?*
newspaper	*el periódico*
thank you	*gracias*
you're welcome	*de nada*
table	*la mesa*
window	*la ventana*

Workers and Workplaces

INSTRUCTIONS   Where do these people work? Write in the Spanish name of the corresponding workplace below the picture of each worker. Check your answers in Appendix A, on page 257.

ACTIVITY 25 • EL TRABAJO: MATCHING

el cartero

1. ....

el camarero

2. ....

el tendero

3. ....

la bibliotecaria

4. ....

el panadero

5. ....

117

ACTIVITY 25 • EL TRABAJO: MATCHING POWER-GLIDE SPANISH JUNIOR I

el bombero

6. ....

la banquera

7. ....

el granjero

8. ....

el maestro

9. ....

el policía

10. ....

ACTIVITY 25 • EL TRABAJO: MATCHING

Translating Descriptions

INSTRUCTIONS You are going to listen to several sentences about what these workers do while they are working. Listen to each sentence and write out its translation in English. Check your answers in Appendix A, on page 257.

1. *El cartero* carries *las cartas* to *las casas*.

   ....

2. *El banquero trabaja* with *mucho* money.

   ....

3. *El policía habla* with *los niños*.

   ....

4. *El maestro escucha a los estudiantes.*

   ....

5. *El granjero camina en la pastura* with *los animales*.

   ....

Identify the Word

INSTRUCTIONS Fill in the blanks with the appropriate word. Check your answers in Appendix A, on page 257.

1. _____ *trabaja en la escuela con los estudiantes.*
2. *El policía trabaja en* _____ .
3. *El banquero* _____ with *muchas personas en el banco.*
4. *El bibliotecario* _____ "Shh! Shh!" *en la biblioteca* when *es muy ruidoso.*
5. _____ *trabaja en el restaurante.*

Listening Practice

INSTRUCTIONS Listen to the following paragraph to figure out the words that are missing. Fill in the blanks with the words that you hear. Listen carefully as the paragraph is read three times. Check your answers in Appendix A, on page 257.

Hay muchos 1._____ *en la ciudad. El panadero trabaja en* 2._____ *y es muy ocupado todos los días. También, el panadero* 3._____ *el pan en* the oven. I love *el pan. Yo como* 4. _____ from *la panadería todos los días.* 5. ¡_____ *excelente!*

Performance Challenge

Individual   Choose one of the workplaces from the list and draw a picture below of what that workplace looks like in your hometown. For example, you could draw a picture of the local police station. Describe the workers who work there and what goes on at that workplace.

My Workplace Drawing

Performance Challenge

Group   On big pieces of paper write the Spanish words of each worker and workplace. Place the papers on the ground in a scattered fashion. Have students choose two papers at a time in an attempt to match the workplace with the worker.

… ACTIVITY 26 • ON THE JOB

On the Job

ACTIVITY 26

In a Restaurant

INSTRUCTIONS   Follow along as you listen to the story. Listen for the main points and then answer the questions.

Vamos al restaurante y vamos a escuchar a la gente. "Bienvenidos a 'La Casa de Carlos.' Hay mucha comida excelente hoy pero las enchiladas son magníficas." Las personas se sientan y el camarero va a la cocina. Las personas, Jorge y María, hablan de la comida. "¿Qué quieres comer?" "Me gustarían el pollo y las papas," dice Jorge. María dice, "Me gusta todo. Yo quiero comer las enchiladas y el arroz." "Perdón, señor. Necesito un menú." El camarero, Ramón, va a la cocina y regresa con el menú. "Muchas gracias," dice María. "De nada," dice Ramón. "Mira, el camarero es muy cortés," dice Jorge.

In this activity you will:
→ Improve your Spanish listening comprehension and reading skills with a short passage and related questions.

Disc **2**   Track **8**

Comprehension Check

INSTRUCTIONS   Answer the following comprehension questions. Check your answers in Appendix A, on page 257.

1. What is being described?

   ....

2. What is the name of the place?

   ....

3. What do they want to eat?

   ....

4. Who is *Ramón*?

   ....

A Few New Words

INSTRUCTIONS   Listen to and learn these words so that you can better understand the restaurant scene that you just listened to.

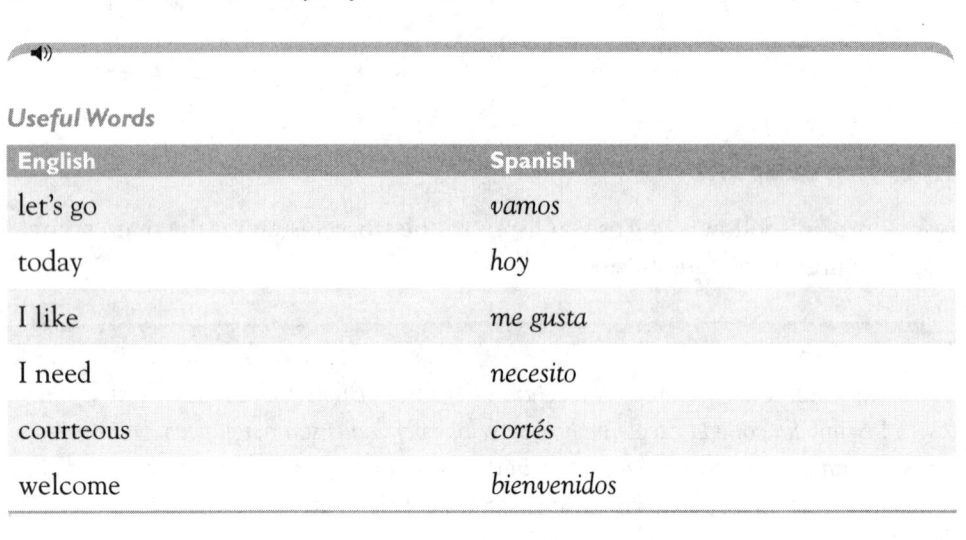

Useful Words

English	Spanish
let's go	vamos
today	hoy
I like	me gusta
I need	necesito
courteous	cortés
welcome	bienvenidos

Jobs in Spanish-speaking Countries

Jobs in Spanish-speaking countries are similar to jobs in other countries in many ways. There are people that grow food and take care of animals, people that make clothes and sell clothes, people that work in cities, and people that work on farms and ranches. With every job, it is important that you show up on time, do your best, have a personality that is easy to work with, and are polite. It is always a good idea to be on your "best behavior" when you are working.

If you could choose one job to do every day, what would it be?

....

Why would you choose that job?

....

....

....

Do you think there is a job similar to the job you want in Spanish-speaking countries?

....

....

How do you think it might be different?

ACTIVITY 26 • ON THE JOB

Performance Challenge

Individual 1 Have you ever had a job to do? Have you ever helped someone or been in charge of finishing something on your own? Make a list of jobs/projects that you have worked on.

Performance Challenge

Individual 2 Go back and read the restaurant scene out loud. If you can, find someone to read the parts with you. Make sure that you practice reading in your best Spanish accent.

Performance Challenge

Group In small groups, act out a restaurant scene like the one in this activity. Use the vocabulary you know to create your own dialogue.

Create a Story

INSTRUCTIONS Write a short story using the words from the list below. You don't have to use all of the words, you just have to be creative!

Word Choices

trabaja	es
mira	habla
dice	tranquilo
¿Dónde está?	viene
perdón	gracias
bienvenidos	de nada
un momento por favor	¿Puedo ayudarle?
el panadero	la panadería
el bombero	el cuerpo de bomberos
la banquera	el banco
el maestro	la escuela

In this activity you will:
- Use the Spanish vocabulary and grammar skills you have acquired so far to write your own short story.

ACTIVITY 27 • CREATE A STORY

Performance Challenge

Individual Practice your story out loud several times and when you are ready, read/perform it out loud for someone else.

Performance Challenge

Group In small groups, create a comic strip showing people ordering and eating in a restaurant. Be creative and make it funny!

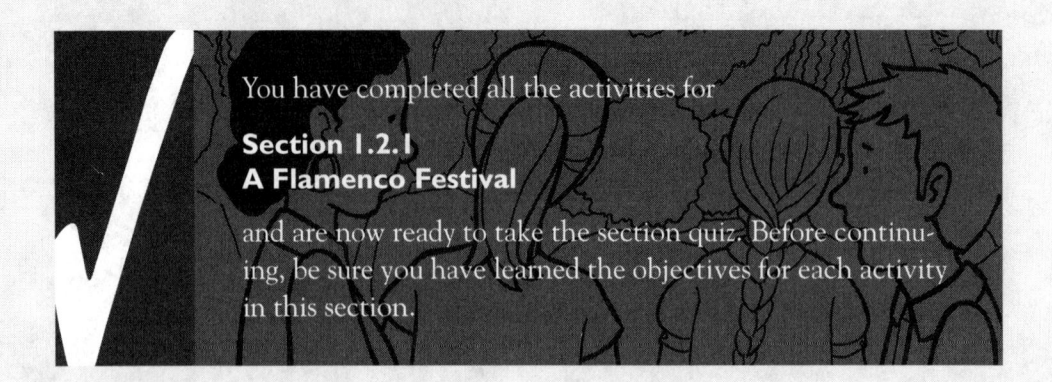

> You have completed all the activities for
> **Section 1.2.1**
> **A Flamenco Festival**
> and are now ready to take the section quiz. Before continuing, be sure you have learned the objectives for each activity in this section.

Disc **2**   Track **9**

Section 1.2.1 Quiz

INSTRUCTIONS   Think about your favorite jobs and where they happen. You are going to send a postcard to a friend or family member telling them about the jobs that you know. Check your answers in Appendix A, on page 264.

Querido (dear) _____,

¡Hola! ¿Cómo 1._____? (How are you?) *Estoy muy bien. Yo estoy aprendiendo sobre los* 2._____ (jobs). *Yo quiero trabajar como un* 3._____ (banker). *Los* 4._____ (bankers) *trabajan en el* 5._____. (bank) 6._____ (there are) *muchos trabajos y me gustan todos.*

¡Adiós!

_____
(your Spanish name)

SECTION 1.2.1 • A FLAMENCO FESTIVAL

INSTRUCTIONS Listen to the following sentences about jobs and match them to the correct pictures. You will hear each sentence twice. Write the number of the sentence below the picture that it matches.

7. _____

8. _____

9. _____

10. _____

11. _____

127

INSTRUCTIONS Write your own sentences. Choose the appropriate subject, verb, and ending from each list to make five sentences. Each word in the table will be used once.

Sentence Elements

A—Subjects	B—Present Tense Verbs	C—Endings
el policía	trabaja	en la panadería
el bibliotecario	habla	en la comisaría
el banquero	trabaja	a los estudiantes
el maestro	dice	en el banco
el panadero	trabaja	"Shh! Shh!"

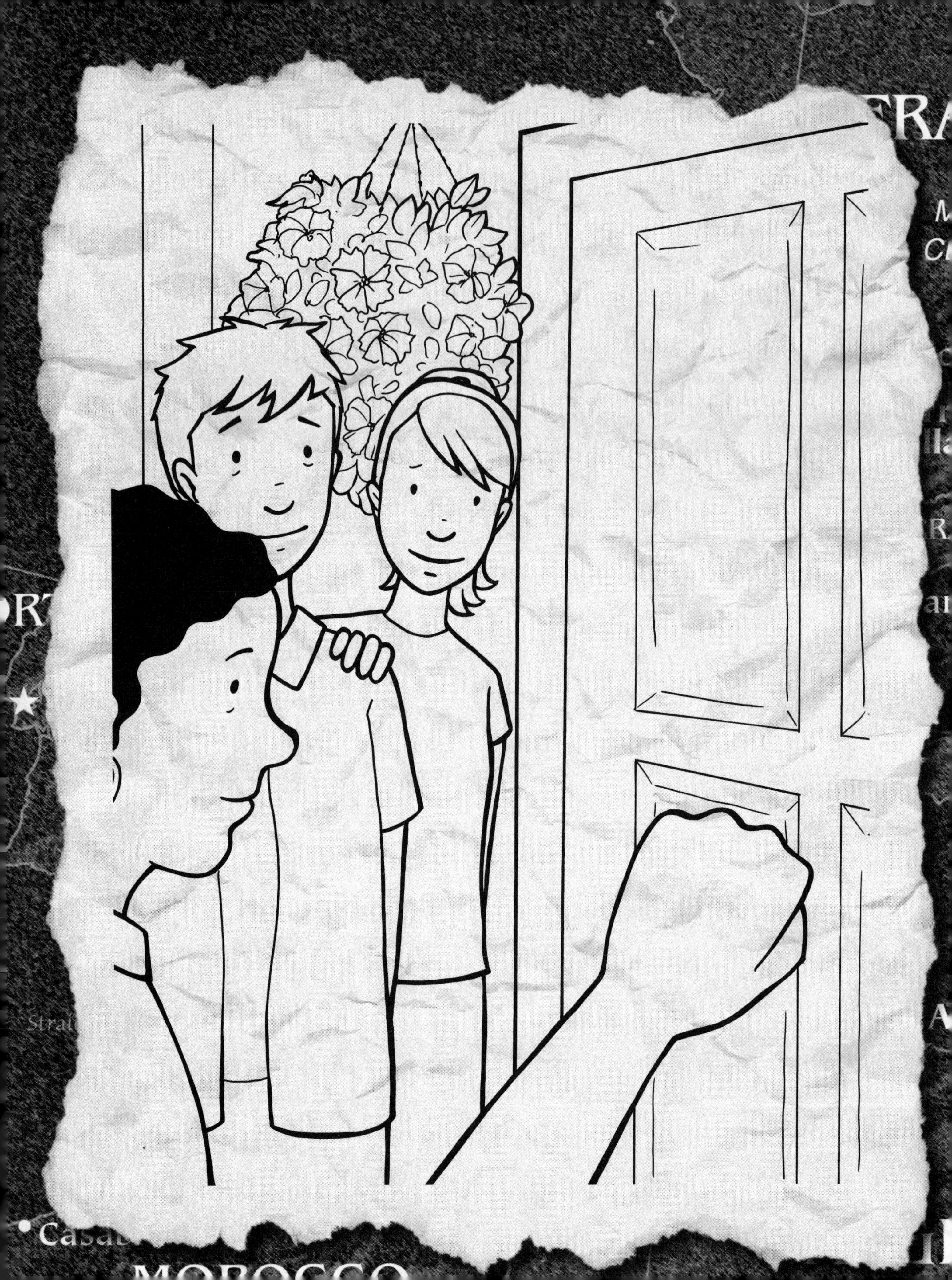

A Few Close Calls

SECTION 1.2.2

You mull over the clue, *pero sin éxito*, with no success. *Cuando* the estate opens to *el público a las diez*, you *entran* and use *las computadoras* in the estate's visitor's center to get online to do some research.

"Look at this," *dice* Lisa after a few *minutos*. You go over and look at her computer screen. She's found the crest for *la universidad de Madrid*, and you can see that a swan features prominently in the design.

"That makes sense," Tony says. "*Una universidad* is like a pond of thought, and if you work at it, an education can make you a better person—maybe the duckling and swan thing is only a comparison."

"*Bueno, qué* are we waiting for?" you ask. You all pile back into *el auto verde de la inspectora Gutierrez* and begin the trip back to Madrid.

You're not even halfway there, though, *cuando la inspectora*, who's been checking the rear view *espejo* with a worried frown, tells you, "Hold on tight, we've got trouble."

Sin further warning, *la inspectora* begins weaving in and out of traffic. Looking back, you can *ver* a black van with dark tinted *ventanas* following you. "*¿Quién es?*" you ask. "*¿Piensa qué es* Don Traición?"

"*No sé*," *responde la inspectora*. "It could be him, or any of the hundred or so bounty hunters also pursuing *la espada de los caballeros*."

After a hair-raising near miss with a semi truck leaves the road blocked behind you, *la inspectora* checks the rear view *espejo* to make sure the van is no longer following, then exits the highway and conceals her *auto* in an abandoned warehouse. "*Mi auto* can't provide us safe *transporte* anymore," *la inspectora* tells you regretfully. "We'll have to find some other way to *Madrid*."

The *cuatro* of you walk to the nearest train station and board *un tren* bound for *Madrid*. *Cuando* you reach *Madrid*, rather than going to *un hotel*, *la inspectora Gutierrez* has *el taxi* take everyone to an older, pleasant-looking *casa* with whitewashed walls and a red tile *techo*. You knock on *la puerta*, and it is opened by an elderly woman who greets *la inspectora* with a warm *abrazo*.

✓ **In this section you will:**

→ Learn to describe what people of different professions are doing in Spanish.

→ Improve your Spanish speaking skills by learning about telephone conversations in Spanish.

→ Master different telephone conversations in Spanish.

→ Review the Spanish numbers 1-20.

→ Learn the Spanish numbers 21-69.

→ Learn simple time telling in Spanish.

→ Improve your reading, listening, and conversation skills through more telephone conversation practice.

(continued)

Disc **2**   Track **10**

> **In this section you will:**
> - Increase your Spanish vocabulary and improve your reading and listening skills with a pair of telephone interviews and comprehension materials.
> - Learn vocabulary and increase reading comprehension and storytelling skills with the first part of a Diglot-Weave™ story.
> - Improve Spanish grammar skills by learning how to discuss the future in Spanish.
> - Practice what you've learned with listening comprehension passages and matching activities.
> - Consolidate what you've learned by writing a telephone conversation in Spanish.
> - Improve your reading and listening comprehension skills with a passage entirely in Spanish.

"Hola, Señora Panadero," la inspectora greets her, smiling. "¿Podemos pasar la noche aquí?"

"Por supuesto," Señora Panadero answers. She nods and motions for you to come in. "Adelante. Pueden pasar arriba y usar los dormitorios que mis niños ya no usan."

"She says we can stay upstairs, in the rooms her children don't use anymore," explica la inspectora. "They're grown up, with houses of their own. We should be safe here tonight."

After a pleasant noche of rest, you and los otros try to figure out what to do. Tony checks Grandpa Glen's travel journal for anything related to la universidad de Madrid. "All I can find is this," dice Tony. "It says 'Third llave, Profesor Alvarez.'"

You check a directory de la universidad and find el Profesor Alvarez. La inspectora Gutierrez advises you to make an appointment before going to visit him. You'll need to make la cita yourselves, though. La inspectora just got an important phone call from her oficina and needs to go in to meet with her jefe.

"I don't know how to talk on el teléfono en español," Lisa says blankly after la inspectora Gutierrez has left.

"Me neither," you reply, "pero we'd better learn, as rápidamente as we can, if we want to get that third key before those guys who were chasing us ayer."

To contact el profesor, you'll need to learn about telephone calls in Spanish. You'll also need to learn how to make plans and appointments, and you should learn more vocabulary as well.

ACTIVITY 28 • JOURNAL

Journal

ACTIVITY 28

¡Hola estudiantes! Do you remember learning about jobs? One job you didn't learn about was *el periodista*—a journalist or newspaper writer. Do you think that you would like to write stories for a newspaper? Would you like to meet a lot of different people and ask them a lot of questions? Doesn't that sound like an exciting job?

Today you are going to have a chance to be *un periodista!* You are writing a short story for *el periódico* (newspaper) about several jobs in the area.

Describing Pictures

INSTRUCTIONS Here are some photos that the newspaper photographer took. Describe each person and their job. Using the words in the table to help you. Match the subjects with the appropriate verb and ending to describe each photo. Check your answers in Appendix A, on page 258.

In this activity you will:

→ Learn to describe what people of different professions are doing in Spanish.

→ Improve your Spanish speaking skills by learning about telephone conversations in Spanish.

Disc **2**   Track **11**

Sentence Elements

Subjects	Present Tense Verbs	Endings
el bombero	trabaja	con los animales en la granja
el tendero	habla	en el cuerpo de bomberos
la banquera	trabaja	a los estudiantes
el maestro	trabaja	"Hola. ¿Puedo ayudarle?"
el granjero	dice	en el banco

1. ....

....

133

ACTIVITY 28 • JOURNAL   POWER-GLIDE SPANISH JUNIOR I

2. ....
   ....
3. ....
   ....
4. ....
   ....
5. ....
   ....

The Telephone

Have you ever used a telephone? _____

How often do you talk on the telephone? _____

In which job do you think they use the telephone the most? _____

People all over the world use the telephone. The telephone is an easy way to talk to people whether they are across the street or across the world. Have you ever talked to someone in another country on the telephone? You are learning so much Spanish that someday soon you might be able to talk to someone on the telephone in Spanish.

INSTRUCTIONS   Imagine that the phone is ringing and you run to answer it. What would you say first? Of course you would say something like "Hello." Here are several ways to answer the telephone in Spanish. Listen and repeat.

Telephone Greetings

English	Spanish
Hello.	*Hola.*
Another way to say Hello.	*Aló.*
Good morning.	*Buenos días.*
Good afternoon.	Buenas tardes.
Good evening.	Buenas noches.
Another greeting similar to Hello.	Bueno.

Match and Learn

INSTRUCTIONS Listen to the greetings and point to the word in the box that matches what you hear. Remember that all of these are ways to greet people when you answer the phone. Check your answers in Appendix A, on page 258.

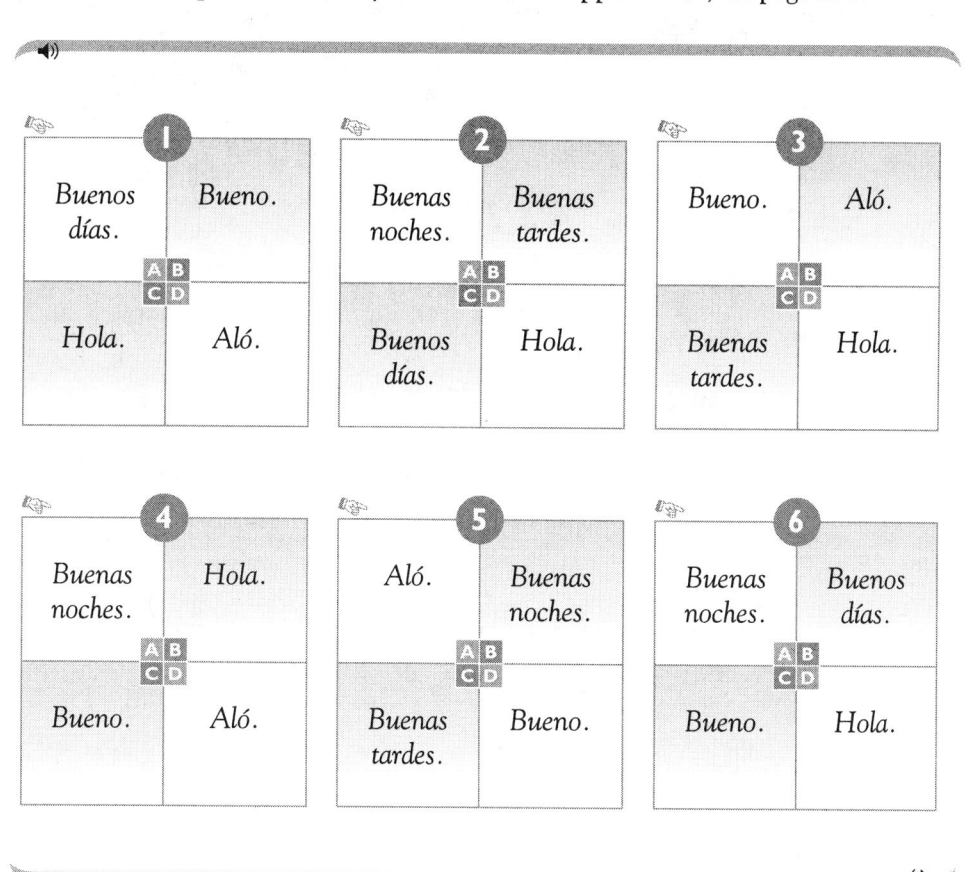

1
A Buenos días.	B Bueno.
C Hola.	D Aló.

2
A Buenas noches.	B Buenas tardes.
C Buenos días.	D Hola.

3
A Bueno.	B Aló.
C Buenas tardes.	D Hola.

4
A Buenas noches.	B Hola.
C Bueno.	D Aló.

5
A Aló.	B Buenas noches.
C Buenas tardes.	D Bueno.

6
A Buenas noches.	B Buenos días.
C Bueno.	D Hola.

Performance Challenge

Individual Interview someone you know about their job. Write up a short newspaper report about the person you interviewed and their job.

ACTIVITY 28 • JOURNAL

135

ACTIVITY 28 • JOURNAL

Performance Challenge

Group In pairs, practice short phone conversations. Use the greetings you know to answer the phone and then use as much Spanish as you can to find out some basic information about the person you are talking to.

El teléfono

ACTIVITY 29

Do you like to talk on the telephone? The phone is a great way to keep in touch with your friends and family and a fun way to find out what is going on.

INSTRUCTIONS Review the ways to greet people when you are answering the phone. Repeat out loud and point to the greeting.

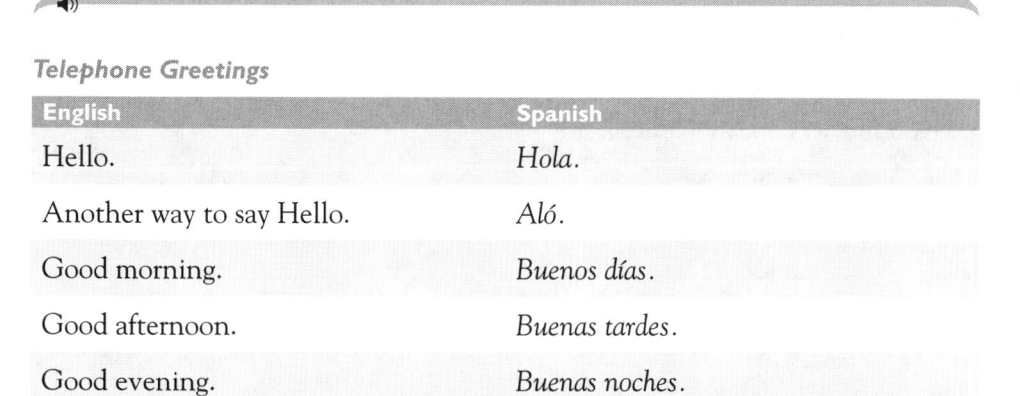

In this activity you will:
→ Master different telephone conversations in Spanish.

Disc **2** Track **12**

Telephone Greetings

English	Spanish
Hello.	Hola.
Another way to say Hello.	Aló.
Good morning.	Buenos días.
Good afternoon.	Buenas tardes.
Good evening.	Buenas noches.
Another greeting similar to Hello.	Bueno.

In order to talk on the phone, you need to learn a few more phrases and how to tell time. Listen to and repeat these phrases.

Phone Phrases

English	Spanish
Is Roberto there?	¿Está Roberto?
One moment please.	Un momento por favor.
What are you doing today?	¿Qué haces hoy?
Would you like to go to _____?	¿Querrías ir a _____?
I like _____.	Me gusta _____.
I am very hungry.	Tengo mucha hambre.
At 12:30.	A las doce y media.
In the afternoon (P.M.).	De la tarde.

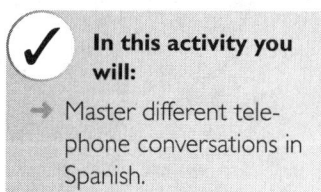

Self Quiz

INSTRUCTIONS   Identify the correct Spanish translation of each of the English phrases you see below. Check your answers in Appendix A, on page 258.

1. **One moment, please.**
   A. *Tengo mucha hambre.*
   B. *Un momento, por favor.*
   C. *De la tarde.*

2. **Would you like to go to _____?**
   A. *¿Querrías ir a _____?*
   B. *¿Está Roberto?*
   C. *¿Qué haces hoy?*

3. **Another way to say Hello.**
   A. *Buenas tardes.*
   B. *Aló.*
   C. *Buenas noches.*

4. **I am very hungry.**
   A. *De la tarde.*
   B. *Aló.*
   C. *Tengo mucha hambre.*

5. **I like ____.**
   A. *Me gusta _____.*
   B. *Tengo mucha hambre.*
   C. *Un momento, por favor.*

6. **Good evening.**
   A. *De la tarde.*
   B. *Buenos días.*
   C. *Buenas noches.*

7. **At 12:30.**
   A. *De la tarde.*
   B. *Tengo mucha hambre.*
   C. *A las doce y media.*

8. **Good morning.**
    A. *Buenos días.*
    B. *Buenas tardes.*
    C. *Buenas noches.*

9. **In the afternoon (P.M.).**
    A. *Un momento, por favor.*
    B. *De la tarde.*
    C. *Buenos días.*

10. **Another greeting, similar to Hello.**
    A. *Bueno.*
    B. *Buenas noches.*
    C. *De la tarde.*

11. **What are you doing today?**
    A. *¿Está Roberto?*
    B. *¿Qué haces hoy?*
    C. *¿Querrías ir a _____?*

12. **Is Roberto there?**
    A. *¿Qué haces hoy?*
    B. *¿Querrías ir a _____?*
    C. *¿Está Roberto?*

13. **Good afternoon.**
    A. *Tengo mucha hambre.*
    B. *Hola.*
    C. *Buenas tardes.*

14. **Hello.**
    A. *Hola.*
    B. *Buenas noches.*
    C. *De la tarde.*

Performance Challenge

Individual   Write out in Spanish a possible conversation you might have with one of your friends. Use as much Spanish as you can.

Performance Challenge

Group   Work in small groups to practice talking on the phone. Students should use the new vocabulary in this activity to invite another student to eat lunch with them.

Numbers and Telling Time

The meaning of "on time" varies from culture to culture. In some cultures, being on time is very important. In other countries and cultures, people aren't very concerned about being on time. For example, in Spain people tend to arrive for events exactly on time. In *México,* "on time" can mean within fifteen minutes of the time they say. And in *Perú,* you may arrive at a party at 10:00 P.M. when it started at 8:00 P.M. This idea of time is often called the *"hora latina."*

In *México* and other Spanish-speaking countries, it is said that family and friends are more important than time. So if a long-lost friend or a family member comes to visit, a person in *México* may not be very worried about being on time to their job or other plans.

Sometimes it is hard for people of different cultures to adjust to being "on time" in countries that they visit. Time is just one more of the interesting differences between cultures.

In this activity you will:
- Review the Spanish numbers 1–20.
- Learn the Spanish numbers 21–69.
- Learn simple time telling in Spanish.

Disc **2**   Track **13**

Numbers

When you are telling time you really need to know numbers 1–12 well and also numbers 1–60. Take a look at those numbers now.

INSTRUCTIONS   Listen and repeat to review numbers 1–20.

uno, dos, tres, cuatro, cinco, seis, siete, ocho, nueve, diez, once, doce, trece, catorce, quince, dieciséis, diecisiete, dieciocho, diecinueve, veinte

Counting Up From 20

Now you are going to learn numbers 20–60. The good part is that numbers are very easy after you know 1–20. There are two ways of spelling out double digit numbers. One way writes out all the numbers separately and uses "y" ("and") to connect them. The other way combines all the numbers together into one word. The "y" is replaced with "i" when the number is spelled out as one word.

INSTRUCTIONS   Learn how to count up from 20 by listening as the following chart is read. Read the numbers again on your own to practice counting and pronouncing the numbers in Spanish.

Counting Up From 20

Three Words	One Word	Numeral
	veinte	20
veinte y uno	veintiuno	21
veinte y dos	veintidós	22
veinte y tres	veintitrés	23
veinte y cuatro	veinticuatro	24
veinte y cinco	veinticinco	25
veinte y seis	veintiséis	26
veinte y siete	veintisiete	27
veinte y ocho	veintiocho	28
veinte y nueve	veintinueve	29

Do you see that you say *veinte* (20) in each number and then you add *uno* (1) through *nueve* (9) after it?

Numbers 30 Through 60

INSTRUCTIONS   Now to get from 30–60 you do the same thing as you do with *veinte*, you add 1–9 after the main number. You only need to learn 4 more words to count up to 60. ¡Qué fácil! Repeat the following numbers.

From 30 to 60

Spanish	Numeral
treinta	30
cuarenta	40
cincuenta	50
sesenta	60

Now add *uno* (1) through *nueve* (9) after *treinta* (30) through *sesenta* (60). Repeat the following numbers.

Counting Up From 30, 40, 50, and 60

Treinta	Cuarenta	Cincuenta	Sesenta
treinta y uno	cuarenta y uno	cincuenta y uno	sesenta y uno
treinta y dos	cuarenta y dos	cincuenta y dos	sesenta y dos
treinta y tres	cuarenta y tres	cincuenta y tres	sesenta y tres
treinta y cuatro	cuarenta y cuatro	cincuenta y cuatro	sesenta y cuatro
treinta y cinco	cuarenta y cinco	cincuenta y cinco	sesenta y cinco
treinta y seis	cuarenta y seis	cincuenta y seis	sesenta y seis
treinta y siete	cuarenta y siete	cincuenta y siete	sesenta y siete
treinta y ocho	cuarenta y ocho	cincuenta y ocho	sesenta y ocho
treinta y nueve	cuarenta y nueve	cincuenta y nueve	sesenta y nueve

¿Qué hora es?—What Time Is It?

We are such busy people and we always need to know what time it is. Repeat the following question. *¿Qué hora es?* What time is it? When someone asks you, *¿Qué hora es?* you will answer the time that it is right now. For example, if it were 8:30 you would say, "*Son las ocho y media.*" *Ocho* for 8 and *media* for a half hour past, or 30 minutes. The time would be 8:30. Telling time is very easy when you know your numbers.

INSTRUCTIONS Learn the following phrases that will help you answer and ask questions about time. Listen and repeat each word and phrase as it is read.

Useful Phrases for Telling Time

English	Spanish
What time is it?	¿Qué hora es?
Quarter of an hour, or 15 minutes	Y cuarto
Half of an hour, or 30 minutes	Y media
Quarter of an hour before that number, or 15 minutes before the hour	Menos cuarto
In the morning (A.M.)	De la mañana

Useful Phrases for Telling Time (cont.)

English	Spanish
In the afternoon (P.M.), from noon to about 6 P.M.	De la tarde
In the evening (P.M.), from about 6 P.M. to midnight	De la noche

Now here are some examples of how to use the phrases you've just learned. Some of them can be tricky so pay attention!

Examples of Telling Time

Time	Spanish
8:15	Son las ocho y cuarto.
8:30	Son las ocho y media.
8:45	Son las nueve menos cuarto.
10:30	Son las diez y media.
9:15	Son las nueve y cuarto.
11:45	Son las doce menos cuarto.
2:10	Son las dos y diez.

Remember when you use "menos cuarto" you have to use the next hour.

ex. We said 11:45 so we had to say *doce* (twelve) *menos cuarto* (minus a quarter of an hour) to get 11:45.

A.M. and P.M.

Now you will learn about A.M. and P.M.

Morning, Afternoon, and Night

Time	Spanish
7:00 A.M.	Son las siete de la mañana.
9:05 P.M.	Son las nueve y cinco de la noche.
3:30 P.M.	Son las tres y media de la tarde.
10:35 A.M.	Son las diez y treinta y cinco de la mañana.

INSTRUCTIONS Imagine that you are looking at your clock and you see these times. Write in the correct time for each and then say them out loud. Check your answers in Appendix A, on page 258.

Your Translation

Time	Spanish Translation
10:45 A.M.	
2:30 P.M.	
8:25 P.M.	
4:15 P.M.	
7:10 A.M.	
6:18 A.M.	
11:38 P.M.	

Performance Challenge

Individual Write down your daily schedule. In Spanish, write out the times that you do certain activities during the day.

Performance Challenge

Group Play "Around the World" with telling time vocabulary words. The teacher will call out a time and two students will try to correctly translate the time into Spanish. The student who loses sits down and another student comes up to challenge the winner.

ACTIVITY 31 • HABLANDO POR TELÉFONO   POWER-GLIDE SPANISH JUNIOR 1

Hablando por teléfono

ACTIVITY 31

✓ **In this activity you will:**
→ Improve your reading, listening, and conversation skills through more telephone conversation practice.

Disc **2**   Track **14**

INSTRUCTIONS ¡Vamos! Listen to this phone conversation and see what you hear.

Carlos Calls Roberto

Spanish
•: Aló.
••: Hola. ¿Está Roberto?
•: Sí, un momento por favor. Roberto teléfono.
••: Roberto, es tu amigo, Carlos. ¿Cómo estás hoy?
•••: Muy bien, gracias. ¿Qué haces hoy?
••: ¿Querrías ir a la cafetería para comer?
•••: Sí. Me gusta comer en la cafetería y tengo mucha hambre. ¿A qué hora vamos?
••: Vamos a la cafetería a las doce y media de la tarde. Nos vemos.
•••: Hasta luego Carlos.

Comprehension Check

INSTRUCTIONS Now read the following questions and listen again. When you hear the conversation this time, listen and look for answers to the following questions. Check your answers in Appendix A, on page 258.

1. Who is calling Roberto?

   ....

2. How is Roberto today?

   ....

3. What does Carlos want to do?

   ....

4. When are they going to eat?

   ....

After you have answered these questions, read the phone conversation out loud on your own. Try to find someone to read one of the parts with you or read each part in a different voice.

More Phone Phrases

Here is a reminder of some important phrases to use and listen for in a phone conversation. Remember that the names can be changed to match your conversation.

INSTRUCTIONS   Listen to and repeat these phrases.

Phone Phrases

English	Spanish
Is Roberto there?	¿Está Roberto?
One moment, please.	Un momento, por favor.
What are you doing today?	¿Qué haces hoy?
Would you like to go to _____?	¿Querrías ir a _____?
I like _____.	Me gusta _____.
I am very hungry.	Tengo mucha hambre.
At 12:30.	A las doce y media.
In the afternoon (P.M.).	De la tarde.

Your Own Phone Conversation

INSTRUCTIONS   Go through the conversation and change the names and places to a conversation you might have with one your friends. Change the underlined words and fill in the blanks to fit your own conversation.

Your Phone Conversation

	Spanish
•:	Aló.
••:	Hola. ¿Está _____?

Your Phone Conversation (cont.)

	Spanish
•:	Sí, un momento por favor. _____, teléfono.
••:	_____, es tu amigo, _____. ¿Cómo estás hoy?
•••:	Muy bien, gracias. ¿Qué haces hoy?
••:	¿Querrías ir a/al _____ para comer?
•••:	Sí. Me gusta _____ y tengo _____. ¿A qué hora vamos?
••:	Vamos a/al _____ a las doce y media de la tarde. Nos vemos.
•••:	Hasta luego _____.

Performance Challenge

Individual Read the phone conversation you've written out loud. Find someone to read the other parts with you and have fun on the phone!

Performance Challenge

Group Work in small groups. Group members sit in a circle and take turns asking a question of the student sitting to their right or responding to the questions of the student on their left. Go around the circle several times before finishing the conversation.

El periodista en el teléfono

Now is your chance to use *el teléfono*. You are going to be a *periodista* (journalist) and call people for interviews.

In your interviews you will need to speak with respect to people you don't know, people who are in positions of authority, and people who are older than you. Examples of people in authority are policemen, teachers, judges, preachers, and others. When you are speaking with respect, you should not use *"tú,"* which is the informal way of saying "you." Instead you should use *"usted"* (ooh stehd), which is the formal way of saying "you." Here are some examples. If you are talking to the following people, you might use these greetings and questions.

Tú and usted

Person	English Greeting	Spanish Greeting
El policía	How are you (formal)?	¿Cómo está usted?
Tu amigo	How are you (informal)?	¿Cómo estás?
El maestro	Good day, Sir. How are you (formal)?	Buenos días, Señor. ¿Cómo está usted?
Tu hermana	Hello. How are you (informal)?	Hola. ¿Cómo estás?

There are many different times when you will use the formal *usted*. You will use *usted* when you are talking to people you don't know and people in positions of authority. You will use the friendly *tú* with your friends and family. When you are reading Spanish, you will now know the difference and importance of both *tú* and *usted*.

In this activity you will:

→ Increase your Spanish vocabulary and improve your reading and listening skills with a pair of telephone interviews and comprehension materials.

Disc **2**   Track **15**

Phone Interview with Martín

INSTRUCTIONS Listen to a few phone interviews and learn some tips.

Martín's Phone Interview

Spanish
•: Bueno.
••: Buenos días Martín. Me llamo José y soy un periodista. Yo trabajo para el periódico. Yo querría preguntarle unas preguntas de su trabajo.
•: Está bien.
••: Bueno. ¿Dónde trabaja usted?
•: Yo trabajo en la panadería.
••: ¿A qué hora va a la panadería cada día?
•: Yo voy a la panadería a las cinco de la mañana.
••: ¿Por qué va al trabajo muy temprano por la mañana?
•: Necesito cocinar el pan, los dulces, y todo antes de que la gente venga para comer.
••: ¿Le gusta trabajar en la panadería?
•: Sí, me gusta mucho. Es interesante y divertido. ¡También, me gusta comer el pan!
••: Muchas gracias. Qué tenga un buen día.

Now read the interview out loud on your own. Try reading the two parts using different voices. Go through the interview and underline all the words you already know. Using the words that you underlined, see if you can come up with the general idea of the interview. After you have done that, look at the list below to help you to understand even more of the interview.

Interview Vocabulary

English	Spanish
the newspaper	el periódico
I would like…	Yo querría…
some questions	unas preguntas
Do you like working?	¿Le gusta trabajar?

Interview Vocabulary (cont.)

English	Spanish
early	*temprano*
I need to cook/bake.	*Necesito cocinar.*
Where?	*¿Dónde?*

Comprehension Check I

INSTRUCTIONS   Now that you have a pretty good idea of what is happening in this interview, answer these questions. Check your answers in Appendix A, on page 258.

1. What does *José* do for work?

   ....

2. Where does *Martín* work?

   ....

3. What time does *Martín* go to work each day?

   ....

4. Why does *Martín* like his job at the bakery?

   ....

Phone Interview with María

INSTRUCTIONS   Now you are going to hear an interview with *María Garcia*. Listen and follow along.

María's Phone Interview

Spanish
•: *Aló. La familia Garcia.*
••: *Hola. ¿Está María?*
•: *Sí. Soy María. ¿Quién es usted?*
••: *Hola María. Me llamo José y soy un periodista. Yo trabajo para el periódico. Yo querría preguntarle unas preguntas de sus animales.*
•: *Bueno, me encantan mis animales.*
••: *María, ¿Qué animales tiene usted?*

María's Phone Interview (cont.)

Spanish
•: Yo tengo muchos animales. Yo tengo dos perros, cinco caballos, una vaca, y ocho ovejas.
••: ¿Cuál es su animal favorito?
•: Yo no tengo un animal favorito porque me encantan todos.
••: ¿Dónde viven los caballos?
•: Mis caballos viven en la pastura y corren mucho.
••: ¿Cómo se llaman sus perros?
•: Mis perros se llaman Sadie y Kacey.
••: Muchas gracias. Qué tenga un buen día. Adiós.
•: Hasta luego.

As you did before, read the interview out loud, read each of the parts using a different voice, and underline all the words you know in the interview. Can you figure out the general idea of the interview? Use this list to help you understand even more of the interview.

Interview Vocabulary

English	Spanish
Who are you (formal)?	¿Quién es usted?
I love	Me encantan
Which?	¿Cuál?
What are their names?	¿Cómo se llaman?

Comprehension Check II

INSTRUCTIONS Now that you have a pretty good idea of what is happening in this interview, answer these questions. Check your answers in Appendix A, on page 258.

1. What animals does *María* have?

   ....

2. How many sheep?

   ....

3. Where do the horses live?

   ....

4. What kind of animals are Sadie and Kacey?

   ....

Performance Challenge

Individual Read a newspaper article and make a list of questions the reporter probably asked in order to find out the information written in the article.

....

....

....

....

....

....

....

....

....

....

....

....

....

....

Performance Challenge

Group Have students interview each other to find out what kinds of animals they have had as pets or that they would like to have.

El patito feo: parte I

ACTIVITY 33

In this activity you will:
- Learn vocabulary and increase reading comprehension and storytelling skills with the first part of a Diglot-Weave™ story.

Disc **2**   Track **16**

INSTRUCTIONS Listen to the following vocabulary words from the story of *El patito feo*.

Vocabulary

English	Spanish
once upon a time	*había una vez*
the farm	*la granja*
family	*familia*
duck	*pato*
morning	*mañana*
six	*seis*
an egg	*un huevo*
small	*pequeño*
the others	*los otros*
but	*pero*
she	*ella*
said	*dijo*
mother	*madre*
ugly	*feo*
pretty	*lindo*
his brothers/brothers and sisters	*sus hermanos*
days	*días*
more and more	*más y más*
and all/everyone	*y todos*

Vocabulary *(cont.)*

English	Spanish
so sad	*tan triste*
poor	*pobre*
nobody	*nadie*
different	*diferente*
my	*mis*
one day	*un día*
birds	*pájaros*
feathers	*plumas*
we	*nosotros*
the ugly duckling	*el patito feo*
pond	*la charca*
goose/geese	*ganso/gansas*
question	*pregunta*
It's dangerous!	*¡Es peligroso!*
men	*hombres*
so/very alone	*tan solo*
old	*viejo*
the old woman	*la vieja*
hens/chickens	*las gallinas*
cat	*el gato*
sleep nor eat	*dormir ni comer*

The Ugly Duckling—*El patito feo: parte I*

INSTRUCTIONS First listen and follow along as the story is read to you. Then read the story out loud on your own to practice reading and speaking Spanish correctly. The English translation is in Appendix A, on page 258.

Había una vez down on an old *granja*, lived a duck *familia*. Mother *Pato* had been sitting on a nest of new eggs for quite some time. One nice *mañana*, the eggs hatched and out popped *seis* little yellow ducklings. *Un huevo* was bigger than the rest, and it didn't hatch. Mother *Pato* couldn't recall laying that large seventh *huevo*. How did it get there? "Tock! Tock!" The *pequeño* prisoner was pecking inside his *huevo*, trying to get out like *los otros* had done.

"Did I not count *los huevos* right?" Mother *Pato* wondered. *Pero* before *ella* had time to think about it, the last *huevo* finally hatched. A strange looking duckling with gray feathers gazed up at a worried *madre*.

The ducklings grew quickly, but *Madre Pato* had a secret worry. "I can't understand how this *feo* duckling can be one of mine!" *dijo ella* to herself. The gray duckling didn't look like *los otros niños* and he certainly wasn't *lindo*. He ate much more than *sus hermanos* and was quickly outgrowing them.

As the *días* went by, the poor *feo* duckling became *más y más* unhappy. *Sus hermanos* didn't want to play with him, he was so clumsy, *y todos* at *la granja* laughed at him. He felt *triste* and lonely. *Madre Pato* did her best to console the poor *feo* duckling. "¡Pobre, pequeño, feo duckling!" *ella* would say. "Why are you so different from *los otros*?" *El feo* duckling secretly cried at night because he was *tan triste*. He felt like nobody wanted him. "*Nadie* loves me, they all tease me! Why am I so *diferente* from *mis hermanos*?"

Un día, he ran away from *la granja*. He stopped at a pond and asked *todos los otros pájaros*. "Do you know of any ducklings with gray *plumas* like mine?" *Pero* everyone shook their *cabezas* in scorn.

"*Nosotros* don't know anyone as *feo* as you." *El patito feo* did not lose heart and went to another *charca*, where a pair of large *gansos* gave him the same answer to his *pregunta*. They also warned him, "Don't stay here! Go away! ¡*Es peligroso*! There are *hombres* with guns around here!" *El patito* was sorry he had left *la granja*. He was scared and *tan solo*, but kept going.

His travels took him near *un viejo* cottage. The old woman who lived in the cottage caught him, thinking he was a stray *ganso*. "I'll put you in the chicken coop so you can lay plenty of *huevos* for me," said *la vieja* whose eyesight was bad. *Pero el patito feo* didn't lay a single *huevo* for *la vieja*. The *gallinas* in the chicken coop didn't like having *el patito feo* around invading their space, so they tried to scare him away. "If you don't lay *huevos*," they *dijeron*, "*la vieja* will cook you up for dinner!" *El gato* that prowled around the coop added, "I hope *la vieja* cooks you, then I can gnaw at your bones!" *El pobre patito feo* was so scared that he could not *dormir ni comer*. He just needed to find a way to get out of there!

Comprehension Check

INSTRUCTIONS Answer the following comprehension questions. Check your answers in Appendix A, on page 259.

1. Why was the *Madre Pato* secretly worried?

   ....

2. How did *el feo* duckling feel "as the *días* went by?"

   ....

3. What did the *gato* hope for?

   ....

Performance Challenge

Individual Tell this part of the story of *El patito feo* to a family member or friend. Practice pronouncing the Spanish words in the story correctly.

Performance Challenge

Group In small groups, create a new part of the story describing an adventure the duckling might have had after he first left the farm. Make up characters for everyone in the group. Act out this new adventure for the rest of the class.

El Futuro: Making Plans

Do you like to talk on the phone? What do you talk about on the phone? Sometimes people talk about things that have already happened. They also often make plans for the future. They have to decide what they want to do, where they want to go, who they want to go with, and so on. It's important to be able to talk about things in the future. Now you need to learn *"ir + a +* verb or a place." This phrase is very common and very useful when making plans. Here's how it works.

- *Voy a* verb/place—is used to say what "I am going to do or where I am going."
- *Vas a* verb/place—is used to say what "you are going to do or where you are going."
- *Va a* verb/place—is used to say what "he/she is going to do or where he/she is going."

Examples of "ir+ a"

English	Spanish
I am going to eat cheese tomorrow.	Yo *voy a comer el queso mañana.*
Marta is going to speak Spanish in the school.	*Marta va a hablar español en la escuela.*
You are going to watch TV tonight.	*Tú vas a mirar la televisión esta noche.*
I am going to work in the bakery for many days.	*Yo voy a trabajar en la panadería por muchos días.*

In this activity you will:

- Improve Spanish grammar skills by learning how to discuss the future in Spanish.
- Practice what you've learned with listening comprehension passages and matching activities.

Disc **2**   Track **17**

Ir + a

The phrase "*ir + a*" will be very helpful when you are making plans with your friends or family, especially on the phone.

INSTRUCTIONS Look at a couple of questions and answers using this new phrase. Listen and follow along.

Phrases Using "ir + a"

English	Spanish
When is Maria going to eat in the cafeteria?	¿Cuándo va a comer María en la cafetería?
Maria is going to eat in the cafeteria at 12 P.M.	María va a comer en la cafetería a las doce de la tarde.
Where am I going to work today?	¿Dónde voy a trabajar hoy?
You are going to work in the house today.	Tú vas a trabajar en la casa hoy.

"Hola Juan."

Now, imagine that you are going to call your *amigo* Juan and plan an outing. Look for the "*ir + a + verb/place*" in this conversation.

INSTRUCTIONS Listen to and read the following conversation.

Calling Juan

	Spanish
•:	Hola Juan.
••:	Hola Carlos.
•:	¿Qué haces?
••:	Yo hablo con mi mamá.
•:	¿Dónde vas a ir mañana?
••:	No sé.
•:	¿Querrías ir a un restaurante mañana?
••:	Sí, vamos al restaurante de Pablo.
•:	¿Qué vas a comer? Yo voy a comer una enchilada y la leche.

Calling Juan (cont.)

Spanish
••: ¡Qué sabroso! Yo voy a comer una quesadilla y unas papas fritas también.
•: Nos vemos mañana.
••: Adiós.

Comprehension Check

INSTRUCTIONS Use your Spanish knowledge to figure out this phone conversation. Check your answers in Appendix A, on page 259.

1. What is Juan doing when Carlos calls him?

2. Where does Juan want to go tomorrow?

3. What is Carlos going to eat at the restaurant?

4. What is Juan going to eat?

Matching

INSTRUCTIONS Match the following Spanish sentences with the English translations. Look carefully at the translations and the Spanish sentences before you make your matches. Write in the letter and the correct English definition to the right of the Spanish sentence. Check your answers in Appendix A, on page 259.

English Translations

English	
A. You run quickly.	B. Ramón is going to speak Spanish.
C. I eat french fries.	D. Ramón speaks Spanish.
E. I am going to eat french fries.	F. You are going to run quickly.

Spanish Sentences

Spanish	Letter/English Definition
1. Ramón va a hablar español.	
2. Yo voy a comer las papas fritas.	
3. Tú vas a correr rápidamente.	

Spanish Sentences *(cont.)*

Spanish	Letter/English Definition
4. *Ramón habla español.*	
5. *Tú corres rápidamente.*	
6. *Yo como las papas fritas.*	

Performance Challenge

Individual In Spanish, make a list of at least 10 things you are going to do today or that you plan to do someday. Use the "*voy a _____*" construction to make your list.

1.
2.
3.
4.
5.
6.
7.
8.
9.
10.

Performance Challenge

Group Plan a trip on your own and then share with a partner what you have planned to do. Use both present tense and "*voy a _____*" constructions to tell your partner what you are going to do on your trip.

Create a Phone Conversation

ACTIVITY 35

In this activity you will:
- Consolidate what you've learned by writing a telephone conversation in Spanish.

INSTRUCTIONS Now is your chance to create your own personal phone conversation. Outline your conversation by answering the following questions.

1. Who do you want to call?

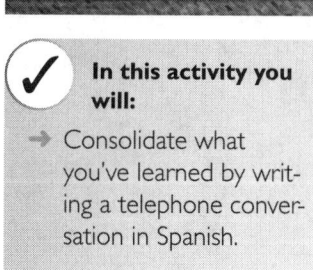

   ....

2. Why do you want to call them?

   ....

3. What are you going to ask them?

   ....

4. What do you want to know?

   ....

Now look back at some of the phone conversations you have listened to and practiced with. Choose greetings, questions, and phrases from them that you want to use. Add your own ideas as well. Try to use as much Spanish as possible.

There is no perfect phone conversation so you're free to be creative. Don't write out your conversation in English first. It is much better to look for thoughts and phrases in Spanish than to write them in English first and then translate. The reason is that many times our thoughts don't translate word for word. *¡Buena suerte!*

....

....

....

....

....

ACTIVITY 35 • CREATE A PHONE CONVERSATION

Performance Challenge

Individual Pay attention to what you say during a normal phone conversation in English. Write down your conversation using as much Spanish as you can.

Performance Challenge

Group Have students practice their phone conversations with other students. Students should practice saying what they have written and also responding to the questions and phrases written by other students.

ACTIVITY 36

Leyendo: Practice Your Reading Skills

In this activity you will:
- Improve your reading and listening comprehension skills with a passage entirely in Spanish.

Disc **2**   Track **18**

Work on reading for correct pronunciation and also on reading to understand the material. First, read this material to practice your Spanish pronunciation and accent. Remember to work hard on pronouncing each word correctly but don't panic on any individual word. Try each one, then move on. Work on reading smoothly and try your best to sound like a "Spanish-speaker." Remember what the native speakers have sounded like on the CD.

INSTRUCTIONS   *¡Vamos!* Relax and enjoy your Spanish! Listen to the story and then read it out loud. The English translation is in Appendix A, on page 259.

Hoy voy a llevar mi perro a mi trabajo. Yo trabajo en una escuela. Soy maestra y mis estudiantes son jóvenes y muy inteligentes. A los estudiantes les gustan mucho los animales y estudian los animales en la clase.

Mi perro se llama Stormy. Stormy tiene siete años y vive en mi granja. A Stormy le gusta correr y jugar con los otros animales. Stormy y yo caminamos y jugamos mucho. Cuando yo monto al caballo, Stormy corre también. Stormy es mi animal favorito.

Stormy va a visitar a mi clase hoy y pienso que los estudiantes van a encantarlo. Los estudiantes pueden correr y jugar con Stormy. Después, vamos a comer el helado y beber la limonada. A Stormy le gusta el helado también.

- Now listen to a native speaker read the first paragraph again. Then you read it out loud, working on your pronunciation. Remember, practice makes perfect!

Hoy voy a llevar mi perro a mi trabajo. Yo trabajo en una escuela. Soy maestra y mis estudiantes son jóvenes y muy inteligentes. A los estudiantes les gustan mucho los animales y estudian los animales en la clase.

Mi perro se llama Stormy. Stormy tiene siete años y vive en mi granja. A Stormy le gusta correr y jugar con los otros animales. Stormy y yo caminamos y jugamos mucho. Cuando yo monto al caballo, Stormy corre también. Stormy es mi animal favorito.

Stormy va a visitar mi clase hoy y pienso que los estudiantes van a encantarlo. Los estudiantes pueden correr y jugar con Stormy. Después, vamos a comer el helado y beber la limonada. A Stormy le gusta el helado también.

Reading to Understand

INSTRUCTIONS This time you don't need to read out loud. Go through the story and underline all of the words that you recognize. When you are finished, see if you can understand the general idea of the story using the words that you already know.

Hoy voy a llevar mi perro a mi trabajo. Yo trabajo en una escuela. Soy maestra y mis estudiantes son jóvenes y muy inteligentes. A los estudiantes les gustan mucho los animales y estudian los animales en la clase.

Mi perro se llama Stormy. Stormy tiene siete años y vive en mi granja. A Stormy le gustan correr y jugar con los otros animales. Stormy y yo caminamos y jugamos mucho. Cuando yo monto al caballo, Stormy corre también. Stormy es mi animal favorito.

Stormy va a visitar mi clase hoy y pienso que los estudiantes van a encantarlo. Los estudiantes pueden correr y jugar con Stormy. Después, vamos a comer el helado y beber la limonada. A Stormy le gusta el helado también.

Identify the sentences that you had trouble understanding. Go through them and circle the words that you need to learn. Now look them up in a dictionary. The key to reading in Spanish is to work with what you already know. It's all right to look up a few unfamiliar words, but don't look up every word. You need to get the general idea without spending all of your time in a dictionary.

Performance Challenge

Individual Write your own story below and record yourself reading it on a tape recorder. Listen to your pronunciation of Spanish and identify ways you can improve.

Performance Challenge

Group Have a "Power Pronunciation" contest. Choose a few words from the Power-Glide Audio Flash Cards and encourage students to pronounce the words correctly and fluently. Have the group vote on who should be named the "Power Pronouncer" of the class.

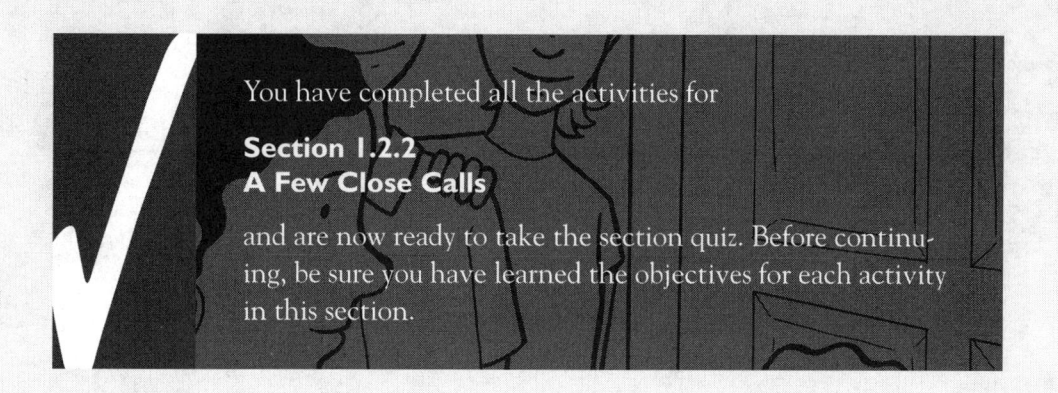

> You have completed all the activities for
>
> **Section 1.2.2**
> **A Few Close Calls**
>
> and are now ready to take the section quiz. Before continuing, be sure you have learned the objectives for each activity in this section.

Section 1.2.2 Quiz

INSTRUCTIONS Before you take the quiz, you will want to practice with all of your flash cards from this lesson. Circle the letter of the English phrase that is a correct translation of the Spanish phrase. Check your answers in Appendix A, on page 264.

1. *¿Está Roberto?*
   A. Would you like to go?
   B. Is Roberto there?

2. *Me gusta _____.*
   A. Is Roberto there?
   B. I like _____.

3. *Menos cuarto*
   A. minus a quarter of an hour or 15 minutes before
   B. half hour or 30 minutes past

4. *Y media*
   A. minus a quarter of an hour or 15 minutes before
   B. half hour or 30 minutes past

5. *¿Querrías ir?*
   A. Would you like to go?
   B. Is Roberto there?

INSTRUCTIONS The following phone conversation is incomplete. In the subsequent questions, choose the word or phrase that best fills the blank in the conversation. Choose the word or phrase that best completes each sentence. Look at the options and write the letter of the correct phrase in the blank.

ex. Vamos __a las doce y media__ de la tarde.

Word Options

Spanish Words		
Bueno.	¿Querrías ir?	menos cuarto
¿Cómo estás?	¿Está Roberto?	vamos
Hasta luego	para comer	al establo
en frente	el caballo	¿Dónde?
al restaurante	al banco	a las doce y media

"6._____" "Hola. 7._____" "Sí, un momento por favor." "Roberto teléfono!" "Hola, es Roberto." "Roberto, es tu amigo, Carlos. ¿Cómo estás hoy?" "Muy bien, gracias. ¿Qué haces hoy?" "¿Querrías ir 8._____ para comer?" "Sí. Tengo mucha hambre. ¿A qué hora vamos?" "Vamos 9._____ de la tarde. Nos vemos."
"10._____ Carlos."

INSTRUCTIONS Think in the future and remember to use "ir + a + verb" in the sentence. Write out the meaning of the English phrase in Spanish.

11. **Julia is going to live in Mexico.**

12. **I am going to eat fruit.**

13. **You are going to talk on the phone.**

INSTRUCTIONS Fill in the blanks with the correct form of *"ir."*

14. *Carlos _____ a hablar en español.*
    Carlos is going to speak in Spanish.

15. *Yo _____ a vivir en la casa.*
    I am going to live in the house.

16. *Tú _____ a mirar la televisión.*
    You are going to watch TV.

✓ You have completed all the sections for
Module 1.2
Before continuing, be sure you have learned the objectives for each activity in this module.

Bay of
Biscay
FRA
Bordeaux
Bilbao
Toulc
Andorr
la Vella
PYRENEES
Porto
Zaragoza
ANDORR
Madrid
RTUGAL
Bar
Tagus
Balearic
Sea
Lisbon
SPAIN
Valencia
Sevilla
Gibraltar
(U.K.)
Málaga
Strait of Gibraltar
Ceuta
(SPAIN)
Alborán
Sea
Oran
Melilla
(SPAIN)
Rabat
Casablanca
ALG

Module 1.3

Keep these tips in mind as you progress through this module:

1. Read instructions carefully.
2. Repeat aloud all the Spanish words you hear on the audio CDs.
3. Learn at your own pace.
4. Have fun with the activities and practice your new language skills with others.
5. Record yourself speaking Spanish on tape so you can evaluate your own speaking progress.

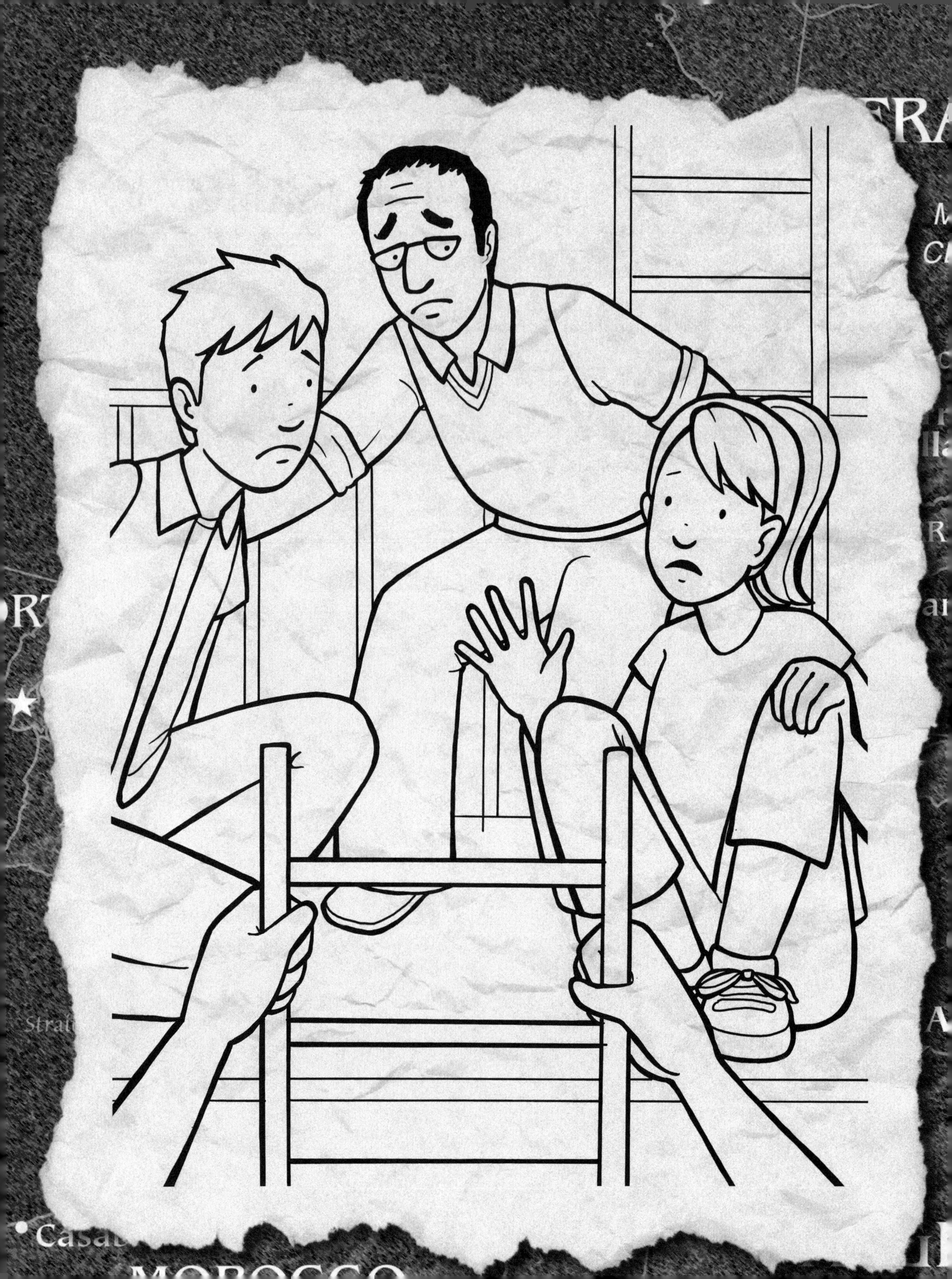

Escape from the University

Tony and Lisa still aren't feeling very confident, so you are the one who gets to call *Profesor Alvarez*. The phone rings several times. You're starting to wonder if he isn't in his *oficina*. Then…

"*¿Aló?*" asks an unfamiliar voice.

"*Hola,*" *respondes*. "*Podría hablar con el Profesor Alvarez.*"

"*Este es el Profesor Alvarez. ¿Quién es usted?*" asks *el profesor*. You give your *nombre*, then Tony's and Lisa's. You ask *el profesor* if he has heard from Grandpa Glen *recientemente*.

"I have been waiting for *ustedes* to call!" *exclama el profesor*. "I can't talk *ahora*, but meet me *hoy*, today, *en mi oficina a las diez y cuarenta y cinco*. That's *un cuarto para las once*, quarter to eleven. *Mi oficina está* in the archaeology building. *¿Está bien?*"

"*Sí, está bien,*" *respondes*. "*¿A qué hora, otra vez?*"

"*Un cuarto para las once,*" *responde el profesor*. "And make certain you're not followed. They know who you are."

You relay the information to Tony and Lisa, then check your watch. It's almost *las diez* now, so if you want to be at *la universidad* by *un cuarto para las once*, you need to leave *inmediatamente*. You can't wait for *la inspectora Gutierrez* to return. You take *un taxi* to *la universidad*. It doesn't take long to find *la oficina del Profesor Alvarez*, and you knock on *la puerta de su oficina* at exactly *un cuarto para las once*. You hear a faint "*Adelante.*" from behind *la puerta*, so you push it open. Behind *la puerta* is a small *oficina* with a large desk, on which are many tall piles of *papeles*.

"*¿Profesor Alvarez?*" Lisa asks timidly.

"*Sí,*" *responde el profesor*, standing up so that you can see him. His dark *cabello* is rumpled, but his *cara* is kind. "You weren't followed, were you?" he asks anxiously. "*Vengan conmigo.* I'll show you where we can talk."

He leads you to the library, *la biblioteca*, and ushers you to a small table with *cuatro sillas* set around it. You all sit down.

In this section you will:

- Learn to apply what you learned about future tense to what you learned about telephone conversations.
- Improve your vocabulary and conversation skills by learning to discuss your daily routine in Spanish.
- Answer questions about vocabulary you have learned.
- Learn a fun game to practice your Spanish vocabulary.
- Learn how to use reflexive verbs in Spanish.
- Increase your Spanish vocabulary and build your listening and reading comprehension skills with the second part of this DiglotWeave™ story.

(continued)

Disc 3   Track 1

SECTION 1.3.1 • ESCAPE FROM THE UNIVERSITY

> **✓ In this section you will:**
> - Learn to compare daily life in the US with daily life in some Spanish-speaking countries.
> - Improve your writing skills and solidify your grammar and vocabulary skills by writing in Spanish about a day in your life.
> - Learn more about reflexive verbs in Spanish.
> - Make posters, using Spanish vocabulary you have learned, that show what you do at different times of the day.

"¿Dónde está the third *llave*? ¿Qué can you tell us about *el caballero* who hid that *llave*?" you ask in a rush.

El Profesor Alvarez hesitates, then quietly *comienza*. "*Lo que* I am going to tell you, only *tres otras personas* living today know, so be very careful about discussing it, even with each other.

"Each *llave* was made and hidden by *uno de los siete caballeros*," *continua el profesor*. "The design and hiding place of each represents something about *el caballero* who was responsible for it. *En el caso* of the third *llave*, *el caballero* who owned it was very fond of..."

He trails off as he looks out of *la ventana*. "We must leave, at once," *dice el profesor* abruptly. "Someone must have tipped them off." You look out of *la ventana* and see a black van parked next to *la biblioteca*. Several *personas* spill out of the van, wearing sunglasses and surgical gloves. They're making a beeline for the entrance three floors below you.

El profesor leads you, Tony, y Lisa to a freight elevator at the back of *la biblioteca*. You take that down *dos* floors, then rush out the *salida de emergencia*, the emergency exit. This leaves you on an old, teetering fire escape. *El profesor* lowers the ladder and helps you to the ground, and you blend in with the crowd of *estudiantes* on the lawn outside until *el grupo* searching *la biblioteca* gives up and leaves.

El Profesor Alvarez drives you back to the police station to report on the *misterioso* van. You see no sign of *la inspectora Gutierrez*, though this is *la oficina* she was supposed to visit. Then *el profesor* takes you back to *la casa de la Señora Panadero*. As he stops *en frente de la casa*, you remind him, "Profesor Alvarez, we still need *información* on the third *caballero* and where to find the third *llave*!"

"I only know *dos cosas*," *responde el profesor*. "*El tercer caballero* loved *todo tipo de animales*. The other is a clue that *mi padre* told me before he died." *El profesor* hastily scribbles it on a scrap of *papel* and hands it to Lisa.

Lisa reads aloud, "*Aquí el gato, la gallina, el pato*, and the goose eat from the same *mano* and sleep with real *ovejas*."

Seeing your puzzled expressions, *el profesor* gives you an encouraging smile. "*Lo siento, pero* that's all I can tell you. ¡Buena suerte!"

You exit *el auto del Profesor Alvarez*, and he drives away. Lisa shakes her head. "Well, I can tell we'll need to do some more studying to figure this one out," *ella dice*.

You'll need to learn about routine and reflexive verbs, and you'll need to master the rest of the story of *el patito* to learn where to find *la tercera llave*.

Journal

ACTIVITY 37

A Phone Conversation

INSTRUCTIONS Listen to and read the following conversation.

Rosa Calls María

Spanish
•: Aló.
••: Hola. ¿Está María?
•: Sí, un momento por favor. ¡María, teléfono!
•••: Hola, es María.
••: María, es tu amiga, Rosa. ¿Cómo estás hoy?
•••: Muy bien, gracias. ¿Qué haces hoy?
••: ¿Querrías ir a la panadería?
•••: Sí. Me gusta comer en la panadería. ¿A qué hora vamos?
••: Vamos a la panadería a las dos y media de la tarde. Nos vemos.
•••: Adiós Rosa.

In this activity you will:
→ Learn to apply what you learned about future tense to what you learned about telephone conversations.

Disc **3**   Track **2**

Comprehension Check

INSTRUCTIONS Answer the following comprehension questions. Check your answers in Appendix A, on page 259.

1. Who is Rosa calling?

   ....

2. Is *María* home?

   ....

3. Where are they going to go?

   ....

4. What time are they meeting to go to *la panadería?*

....

El teléfono

El teléfono can be a great tool. You can use *el teléfono* to call your *amigos*, your *familia*, or anyone else. When you're on the phone, you're probably catching up on what has happened or planning what is going to happen. As you learned in the last lesson, it is important to be able to talk about what is going to happen in the future.

INSTRUCTIONS Take a quick look at "*ir + a +* verb/place" again as you listen to the following sentences. Repeat each phrase after you hear it.

"*Ir + a*"

English	Spanish
I am going to run to the barn.	*Yo voy a correr al establo.*
Luisa is going to talk on the phone.	*Luisa va a hablar por teléfono.*
The horse is going to live in the pasture.	*El caballo va a vivir en la pastura.*
You are going to work at the market.	*Tú vas a trabajar en el mercado.*

Questions and Answers

INSTRUCTIONS Now, answer the following questions that you may be asked during a phone conversation. Use "*ir + a +* verb/place" in each of your answers. Check your answers in Appendix A, on page 260.

ex. *¿Vas a comer la fruta? Sí, yo voy a comer la fruta.*

Or if you aren't going to eat the fruit, you need to use "*no*" twice at the beginning of your answer. *¿Vas a comer la fruta? No, no voy a comer la fruta.*

1. *¿Vas a hablar en español?*

....

2. *¿Vas a vivir en el establo?*

....

3. *¿Vas a trabajar mucho?*

....

Refrán

Here's another *refrán*. Practice saying it out loud several times and try to use it today in a conversation.

Habla poco y escucha mucho.
Literal translation: Speak little and listen much.
Meaning: Speak little; listen much.

4. ¿Vas a correr con los animales?

5. ¿Vas a decir "hola?"

Performance Challenge

Individual Write out a few of the things you are going to do on a busy day. Then, write out a phone conversation you might have with a friend about your busy day.

Performance Challenge

Group Have pairs of students practice talking on the phone with each other. One student should ask questions about what the other student is going to do. Have students switch roles.

ACTIVITY 38 • DAILY ROUTINE POWER-GLIDE SPANISH JUNIOR I

Daily Routine

Many of us do the same things almost every day. We get up in the morning, take a bath, eat breakfast, go to school, play with our friends, and come home again. It's interesting to think that other people are doing exactly the same things that we are doing every day.

INSTRUCTIONS Here are some words you will need to know to be able to talk about people's daily lives. Listen to each word and repeat it out loud.

ACTIVITY 38

In this activity you will:
→ Improve your vocabulary and conversation skills by learning to discuss your daily routine in Spanish.

Disc **3**   Track **3**

Daily Activities

English	Spanish
in the morning	*de la mañana*
in the afternoon	*de la tarde*
in the evening	*de la noche*
later	*después*
I get up	*me levanto*
he/she/formal you get up	*se levanta*
I get dressed	*me visto*
he/she/formal you get dressed	*se viste*
I go	*voy*
he/she/formal you goes	*va*
I go to sleep	*me duermo*
he/she/formal you goes to sleep	*se duerme*
I eat	*como*
he/she/formal you eats	*come*
I play	*juego*
he/she/formal you plays	*juega*

A Daily Routine

INSTRUCTIONS   Listen to this paragraph about what Carla does every day and then read it out loud. Look at the questions so you know what information you are looking and listening for.

En la mañana, me levanto a las siete y me baño. Normalmente, yo como el cereal. Yo voy a la escuela y hablo con mis amigos. Después de la escuela, yo juego con mis hermanos en mi casa. A las seis de la noche, yo como la cena. Yo miro la tele con mi familia y me duermo a las ocho y media de la noche.

Comprehension Check

INSTRUCTIONS   Answer the following comprehension questions. Check your answers in Appendix A, on page 260.

1. What time does Carla get up in the morning?

2. When Carla goes to school, what does she do with her friends?

3. Where does Carla play with her brothers and sisters *(hermanos)*?

4. What does Carla do at 6 P.M.?

5. What does Carla do with her family?

Writing Practice

INSTRUCTIONS   Write the translation of each phrase to the right of the Spanish phrase. Check your answers in Appendix A, on page 260.

Spanish to English

Spanish	English Translation
1. *de la mañana*	
2. *de la noche*	
3. *voy*	

Spanish to English (cont.)

Spanish	English Translation
4. *va*	
5. *como*	
6. *juega*	
7. *se levanta*	
8. *me baño*	
9. *se viste*	
10. *me duermo*	
11. *se duerme*	

Listening Comprehension

INSTRUCTIONS Listen as each word or phrase is repeated twice. In the spaces below, write down the Spanish words and phrases you hear. Check your answers in Appendix A, on page 260.

1.
2.
3.
4.
5.
6.
7.

Performance Challenge

Individual Write down what you do every day and use the new vocabulary words and phrases to describe when you do each of your daily activities.

Performance Challenge

Group Divide the class into teams. Have one student from each team go up to the chalkboard and race to write out the correct Spanish translation of the vocabulary word or phrase the teacher calls out.

What's Happening Today?

In this activity you will:
- Answer questions about vocabulary you have learned.
- Learn a fun game to practice your Spanish vocabulary.

INSTRUCTIONS Circle the letter of the English phrase that is a correct translation of the Spanish. Check your answers in Appendix A, on page 260.

1. *¿Cómo estas?*
   A. How are you?
   B. half past, 30 minutes
   C. I play

2. *y media*
   A. at night (P.M.)
   B. I go to sleep
   C. half past, 30 minutes

3. *de la tarde*
   A. in the afternoon (P.M.)
   B. half past, 30 minutes
   C. at night (P.M.)

4. *juego*
   A. I go to sleep
   B. I play
   C. I go

5. *se levanta*
   A. he/she/formal you gets up
   B. half past, 30 minutes
   C. How are you?

6. *voy*
   A. at night (P.M.)
   B. I play
   C. I go

7. *me duermo*
   A. he/she/formal you gets up
   B. I go to sleep
   C. I play

8. *de la noche*
   A. in the afternoon (P.M.)
   B. at night (P.M.)
   C. I go to sleep

Complete the Conversation

INSTRUCTIONS   Fill in the blanks with the letter of the word or phrase that best completes each sentence. You won't use all the words listed, just the ones that make the most sense in the paragraph. Check your answers in Appendix A, on page 260.

Word Options

Spanish Words		
A. *después*	B. *y media*
C. *de la noche*	D. *como*
E. *hablo*	F. *me duermo*
G. *mañana*	H. *de la tarde*

En la 1._____, me levanto a las siete y me baño. Normalmente, yo 2._____ el cereal. Yo voy a la escuela y 3._____ con mis amigos. 4._____ de la escuela, yo juego con mis hermanos en mi casa. A las seis de la noche, yo como la cena. Yo miro la tele con mi familia y 5._____ a las ocho y media.

Matamoscas

Today you are going to learn to play *Matamoscas*. *Matamoscas* means "flyswatter" and that is what you are going to use in this game. You need two flyswatters and a big piece of paper (poster paper or butcher paper will work well) to write your vocabulary words on. You can use just the vocabulary that you learned in this lesson or you can use any Spanish vocabulary that you know. Scatter the vocabulary words around the paper: sideways, diagonally, up and down, horizontal, etc.

To play *Matamoscas* it works best to have at least 3 people: one to read the vocabulary word, two people to use the flyswatters. You can also play with two teams or practice on your own. Someone will read a vocabulary word from the list (in English) and the two people with the flyswatters will try to find the correct Spanish word on the poster and swat it. Whoever swats the correct word first wins!

Matamoscas is a fun way to learn and review your Spanish vocabulary. You also can make a *Matamoscas* poster for verbs, nouns, phrases, and anything else you are learning. Have fun!

Performance Challenge

Individual   Create your own poster with new vocabulary words on it. Teach a friend or family member a few of these Spanish vocabulary words and play "*Matamoscas*" as described in this activity.

Performance Challenge

Group   Play the game "*Matamoscas*" as a class. Write Spanish words and phrases on the board for students to swat.

Reflexive Verbs

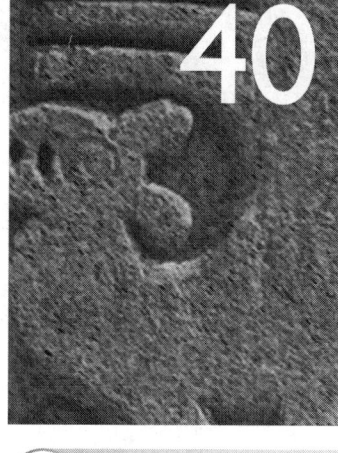

ACTIVITY 40

INSTRUCTIONS Listen as Luisa explains what she does in a day. Then read the following paragraph out loud for pronunciation practice.

En la mañana, me levanto a las seis y media y me baño. Normalmente, yo como el cereal. Yo voy a la escuela y hablo con mis amigos. Después de la escuela, yo juego con mis hermanos en mi casa. A las cuatro y cuarto de la tarde, yo como una tortilla y a las siete de la noche, yo como la cena. Yo miro televisión con mi familia y me duermo a las ocho y media de la noche.

Now listen as someone else tells you about what Luisa does in a day. Then, read the following paragraph out loud.

En la mañana, Luisa se levanta a las seis y media y se baña. Normalmente, Luisa come el cereal. Ella va a la escuela y habla con sus amigos. Después de la escuela, Luisa juega con sus hermanos en su casa. A las cuatro y cuarto de la tarde, ella come una tortilla y a las siete de la noche, Luisa come la cena. Luisa mira televisión con su familia y se duerme a las ocho y media.

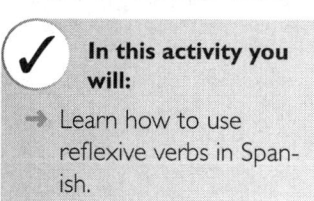

In this activity you will:
- Learn how to use reflexive verbs in Spanish.

Disc **3**   Track **4**

Recognizing Differences

Both of these paragraphs describe Luisa's day, but they are different. Can you recognize the differences between them? Can you see what changed in the second paragraph? You're right! All of the verbs in the second paragraph are talking about Luisa in the third person. Look at these examples. Check your answers in Appendix A, on page 260.

First and Third Person

First Person: English	First Person: Spanish	Third Person: English	Third Person: Spanish
I take a bath	*Me baño*	Luisa takes a bath	*Luisa se baña*
I get up	*Me levanto*	Luisa gets up	*Luisa se levanta*
I eat	*Yo como*	Luisa eats	*Luisa come*
I go	*Yo voy*	She goes	*Ella va*
I talk	*Hablo*	She talks	*Habla*

First and Third Person (cont.)

First Person: English	First Person: Spanish	Third Person: English	Third Person: Spanish
I play	*Yo juego*	Luisa plays	*Luisa juega*
I watch	*Yo miro*	Luisa watches	*Luisa mira*
I get dressed	*Me visto*	Luisa gets dressed	*Luisa se viste*
I go to sleep	*Me duermo*	Luisa goes to sleep	*Luisa se duerme*

Do you see that these words are very similar but are written just a little bit differently? Remember that "*yo*" means "I" and "*ella*" means "she."

INSTRUCTIONS Fill in the blanks with the correct phrase from the list above.

1. *Yo* _____ (I take a bath) *en la mañana.*
2. *Luisa* _____ (gets dressed) *todos los días.*
3. *Luisa* _____ (goes to sleep) *a las nueve de la noche.*
4. *Yo* _____ (get up) *a las siete de la mañana.*
5. *Luisa* _____ (takes a bath) *por la noche.*

Performance Challenge

Individual Write a short paragraph about what you do in a day. Use the paragraph about Luisa in this activity as a pattern.

Performance Challenge

Group Have students work in pairs. Each student will say a few things they do using the words and phrases from this activity. Then, each student will switch partners and explain in the third person a few things their original partner does.

El patito feo: parte II

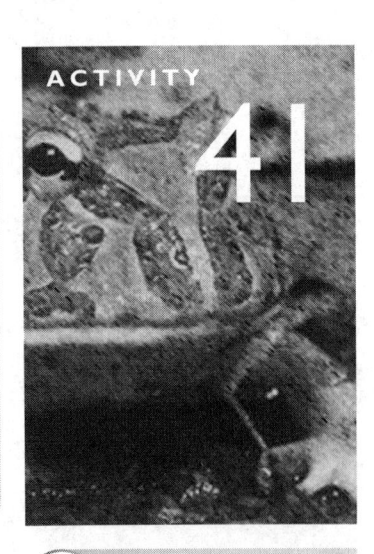

ACTIVITY 41

In this activity you will:
- Increase your Spanish vocabulary and build your listening and reading comprehension skills with the second part of this DiglotWeave™ story.

Disc **3**   Track **5**

INSTRUCTIONS Listen to the following vocabulary words from the story of *El patito feo*.

Vocabulary

English	Spanish
duck	*pato*
morning	*mañana*
said	*dijo*
pretty	*lindo*
poor	*pobre*
nobody	*nadie*
different	*diferente*
my	*mis*
one day	*un día*
birds	*pájaros*
we	*nosotros*
the ugly duckling	*el patito feo*
pond	*la charca*
so/very alone	*tan solo*
old	*viejo*
hens/chickens	*las gallinas*
cat	*el gato*
one night	*una noche*
the door	*la puerta*

Vocabulary *(cont.)*

English	Spanish
food	*comida*
happier	*más feliz*
white	*blanco*
yellow	*amarillo*
big/large	*grande*
winter	*el invierno*
water	*el agua*
a farmer	*un granjero*
cold	*frío*
the farmer's house	*la casa del granjero*
and so	*y así*
when	*cuando*
he	*él*
like	*como*
where	*dónde*
swan	*cisne*
happiness	*felicidad*

The Ugly Duckling—*El patito feo: parte II*

INSTRUCTIONS First listen and follow along as the story is read to you. Then read the story out loud on your own to practice reading and speaking Spanish correctly. The English translation is in Appendix A, on page 260.

Una noche, finding *la puerta* of the chicken coop ajar, *el patito feo* escaped. Once again he was *tan solo,* but at least he wasn't with those mean *gallinas y gato* anymore. He went as far away from the *viejo* cottage as he could, and in *la mañana,* he found himself in a thick bed of reeds. "If *nadie* wants me, I'll hide here forever." There was plenty of *comida* and *nadie* around to scare *el patito feo* and so he began to feel *más feliz,* though he was lonely. *Un día* at sunrise, he saw a group of beautiful *pájaros* flying overhead. They were *blanco,* with long slender necks, *amarillo* beaks, and *grandes* wings.

"If only I could look like them, just for *un día,*" *dijo el patito* admiringly. *El invierno* came *y el agua* in the reed bed froze. *El pobre patito* eventually had to leave his frozen home to search for *comida* in the *frío* snow. He quickly became exhausted *y* fell to the ground. Fortunately, *un granjero* found him *y* put him in his *grande* jacket pocket. "I'll take him home to *mis niños.* They'll look after him. *Pobre* thing, he's frozen!" *El patito* was showered with kindly care at *la casa del granjero.* *Y así, el patito feo* was able to survive the bitterly *frío invierno.*

Cuando por fin Spring had arrived, *el patito feo* had grown so *grande* that *el granjero* decided, "I'll set him free by *la charca.*" *Cuando el patito* swam onto *la charca* he saw his reflection in the water. "I hardly recognize myself," *él dijo.* He really had grown up. He wasn't *un patito* anymore. He wasn't *feo* anymore either. As he sat there examining his reflection in *el agua*, *los pájaros* with the *grande, blanco* wings glided onto *la charca*. *Cuando el patito* saw them, he realized that his reflection matched theirs. He now looked just like them. He was one of their kind!

The beautiful *pájaros* swam near *el patito* and said, "*Nosotros* are swans *como* you. *¿Dónde* have you been hiding? How come *nosotros* have never met you before?" "It's a long story," replied *el patito*, who really wasn't *un pato* at all, but a young *cisne*. He happily made friends with his fellow *cisnes* and swam majestically with them on *la charca*.

Un día, he heard *niños* on the bank exclaim, "Look at that young *cisne*! He's the most *lindo* of *todos los cisnes*!" The young *cisne* almost burst with *felicidad* because now he knew why he had been so *diferente* from *los patos* he had grown up with. He was *un lindo cisne*!

Comprehension Check

INSTRUCTIONS   Answer the following comprehension questions. Check your answers in Appendix A, on page 261.

1. How was *el patito feo* able to survive the *invierno*?

   ....

2. What did *el patito feo* wish for when he saw the birds with the big, white wings?

   ....

3. In the end, what did *el patito feo* discover about himself?

   ....

Performance Challenge

Individual   Use the vocabulary list at the beginning of the story to write your own story. Use as many of the vocabulary words as you can.

Performance Challenge

Group Create a new part of the story that tells about what *el patito feo* did at the farmer's house during *el invierno*.

The U.S. and Spanish-Speaking Countries

Daily life in all parts of the world is similar and yet very different. Take a look at what happens in Spanish-speaking countries every day.

In many Spanish-speaking countries, the subway is used to get around. *El metro, el subterráneo,* and *el subte* are a few ways to say subway in Spanish. Every day, *el metro* transports a lot of people to work, to school, and to visit their families.

The bus, *el autobús,* is another popular form of transportation in Spanish-speaking countries. Buses are not used much in rural parts of the United States, but they are very useful in big cities. *El autobús* is common in Spanish-speaking countries in both the cities and the rural areas. Some people that live in rural areas rely on *el autobús* to get to the market, to get to their job in town, and to travel to see their extended families. Not everyone in the world has a car to get them to where they need to go. There are many more cars per family in the United States than there are in most Spanish-speaking countries.

Not only is walking a common way to get around in Spanish-speaking countries, it is also a way of socializing. Sunday afternoons are especially popular for socializing while walking. You might see families walking together, friends walking and talking or young couples walking hand in hand.

The school day is often longer in Spanish-speaking countries because the students sometimes have up to 10 classes/subjects each day. Did you know that one of the most popular foreign language classes is English? Sports and other activities aren't provided by the school, but kids can participate in them through local clubs. Music and art are a very important part of education in the Spanish-speaking world. Some children even go to special music schools called *"conservatorios"* to focus their studies on music.

La televisión is watched almost worldwide. In Venezuela, many variety shows and *telenovelas* (soap operas) are produced entirely in Spanish. Many of these shows made in Venezuela can be seen on Spanish channels in the United States.

In this activity you will:

→ Learn to compare daily life in the US with daily life in some Spanish-speaking countries.

La Zona Rosa

Here's an interesting fact. In the *Zona Rosa* (a busy and popular eating and entertainment area) in Mexico City, there are policemen that are there to help you with directions. They are called tourist police!

In some Spanish-speaking countries, pharmacies are very different than they are in the United States. Instead of going to the doctor, people go to the pharmacy when they are sick. The pharmacists are able to prescribe and give the needed medication to help people get better. Some pharmacies even have a person there that is able to give shots when people need them.

Performance Challenge

Individual 1   Now it's your turn to describe your daily life. Think about what you and other people you know do and see every day: clothes, food, music, transportation, etc. Write down 5 things that come to mind. Are any of them similar to life in Spanish-speaking countries?

1. ....
2. ....
3. ....
4. ....
5. ....

Performance Challenge

Individual 2   Compare and contrast what you just learned about parts of daily life in Spanish-speaking countries with your own life. Write at least 2–3 paragraphs. Be sure to share your feelings and comments.

Performance Challenge

Group In small groups, have students research the different modes of transportation used in Spanish-speaking countries. Give each group a picture of their assigned form of transportation and some resources to use for their research.

My Day

ACTIVITY 43 • MY DAY

In this activity you will:
→ Improve your writing skills and solidify your grammar and vocabulary skills by writing in Spanish about a day in your life.

INSTRUCTIONS Create a story about a day in your life. Explain what an actual day for you is like, or you can use your imagination and create a "fun" day for yourself.

First, make a list of what you want to do that day. Use some of the words that you already know in Spanish. Fill in the blanks with English when you don't know the Spanish. Try to list between 8 and 10 simple activities.

1. ....
2. ....
3. ....
4. ....
5. ....
6. ....
7. ....
8. ....
9. ....
10. ....

Then, draw 8–10 pictures to match the activities you are planning to do that day.

ACTIVITY 43 • MY DAY

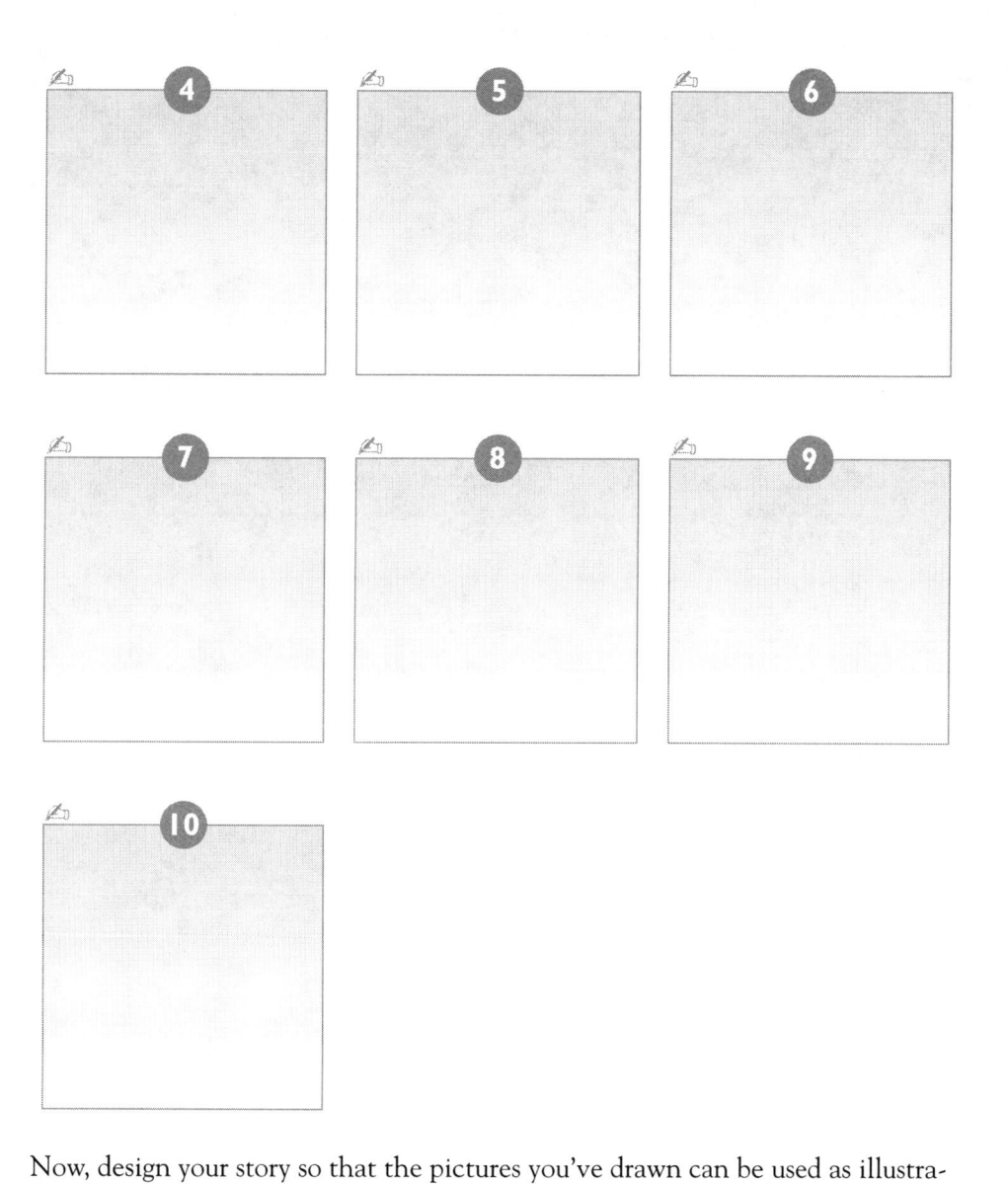

Now, design your story so that the pictures you've drawn can be used as illustrations for the story. Try to keep most of the story in Spanish, using very few English words and phrases.

....

....

....

....

....

....

Performance Challenge

Individual 1 Practice reading your story out loud. Then when you are ready, present it to your classmates, teacher, friends, or family.

Performance Challenge

Individual 2 With the list of activities you made for this activity, create a song about some of the things you do every day. Set your lyrics to music and perform it for your friends or family members.

Performance Challenge

Group Have one student at a time act out or describe in Spanish something that they do every day. Let the class guess what activity the student does daily.

More Reflexive Verbs and Review

In this activity you will:
- Learn more about reflexive verbs in Spanish.

Disc **3**   Track **6**

INSTRUCTIONS   Listen to the following words and then repeat them out loud.

Vocabulary

English	Spanish
I wake up	me despierto
he/she/formal you wakes up	se despierta
I go to bed	me acuesto
he/she/formal you goes to bed	se acuesta
with	con
much	mucho
always	siempre
every day	todos los días

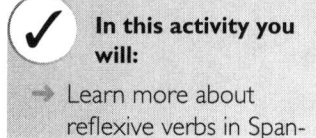

Performance Challenge

Individual   Play a memory game with all of the vocabulary words from this lesson. Use Power-Glide's Flash Cards or make your own. Place the cards face down on the ground and pick them up two at a time until you can make a match.

Performance Challenge

Group Play a memory game as a class using selected vocabulary words and phrases from this lesson. Write words out on the board or create large flash cards for students to remember and match.

Make Posters: What Happens When?

In this activity you will:

→ Make posters, using Spanish vocabulary you have learned, that show what you do at different times of the day.

You are going to make some posters today about what happens *de la mañana, de la tarde, y de la noche*. You do many things each day, but right now focus on what you do in the morning, in the afternoon, and at night. Write the activities under the correct title. Remember that *mañana* is from midnight to noon, *tarde* is from noon to about 6 P.M., and *noche* is from about 6 P.M. to midnight.

Your Daily Activities

De la mañana	De la tarde	De la noche

After you have finished your list, make a poster for each time of day. You need to draw or cut out a picture to go with each of the activities you've listed. These posters should be fun and colorful. They will be a great way to help you remember some Spanish phrases and words. Make sure you practice saying all of the Spanish words out loud as you add them to your list and then your posters. Be creative!

Performance Challenge

Individual Create your own comic strip showing a story line that goes through the different times of the day. Write the dialogue for your comic strip in Spanish and be sure to use the vocabulary from this activity.

Performance Challenge

Group Have groups make posters highlighting what goes on at certain times of the day: *de la mañana, de la tarde, de la noche*. Let each group present their poster to the class.

SECTION 1.3.1 • ESCAPE FROM THE UNIVERSITY

You have completed all the activities for

**Section 1.3.1
Escape from the University**

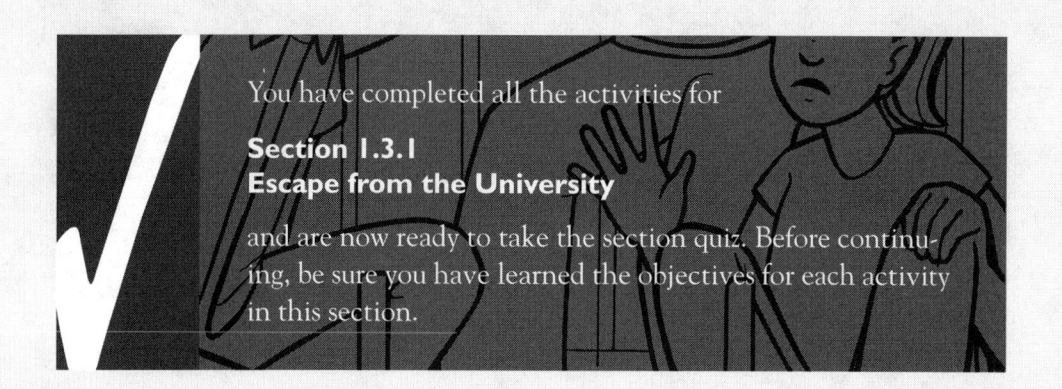

and are now ready to take the section quiz. Before continuing, be sure you have learned the objectives for each activity in this section.

Section 1.3.1 Quiz

INSTRUCTIONS Send a postcard to a friend, teacher, or family member. Tell them about what you do during a normal day in *español*. Fill in the blanks to finish your letter. Check your answers in Appendix A, on page 264.

Querido _____,

Here in Spain we are very busy, but I want to use the Spanish I am learning to describe a normal day for me back at home. *Por la mañana,* 1._____ (I wake up). *Normalmente,* 2._____ (I eat) *el cereal.* 3._____ (I go) *a la escuela y* 4._____ (I talk) *con mis amigos. Después de la escuela,* 5._____ (I play) *con mis hermanos en mi casa. A las siete de la noche,* 6._____ (I eat dinner) 7._____ (I go to sleep) 8._____ (at 9:00).

¡Hasta luego!

_____
(your Spanish name)

INSTRUCTIONS Choose the correct English translation of the Spanish words and phrases. Circle your answers. *¡Buena suerte!*

9. ***Me acuesto***
   A. I eat
   B. I go to bed
   C. I agree

209

10. **Se levanta**
    A. he/she/formal you gets up
    B. they sleep
    C. she leaves

11. **Siempre**
    A. Never
    B. Sometimes
    C. Always

12. **Me baño**
    A. I take a bath
    B. I go to bed
    C. I go to the bathroom

13. **De la tarde**
    A. to be late
    B. in the afternoon
    C. of the day

14. **Ocho y media**
    A. 8:15
    B. 8:45
    C. 8:30

15. **Se viste**
    A. they see
    B. we visit
    C. he/she/formal you gets dressed

16. **Diez y cuarenta**
    A. 10:04
    B. 10:40
    C. 10:14

17. **Todos los días**
    A. always
    B. sometimes
    C. every day

18. **Yo voy**
    A. I go
    B. I eat
    C. I sleep

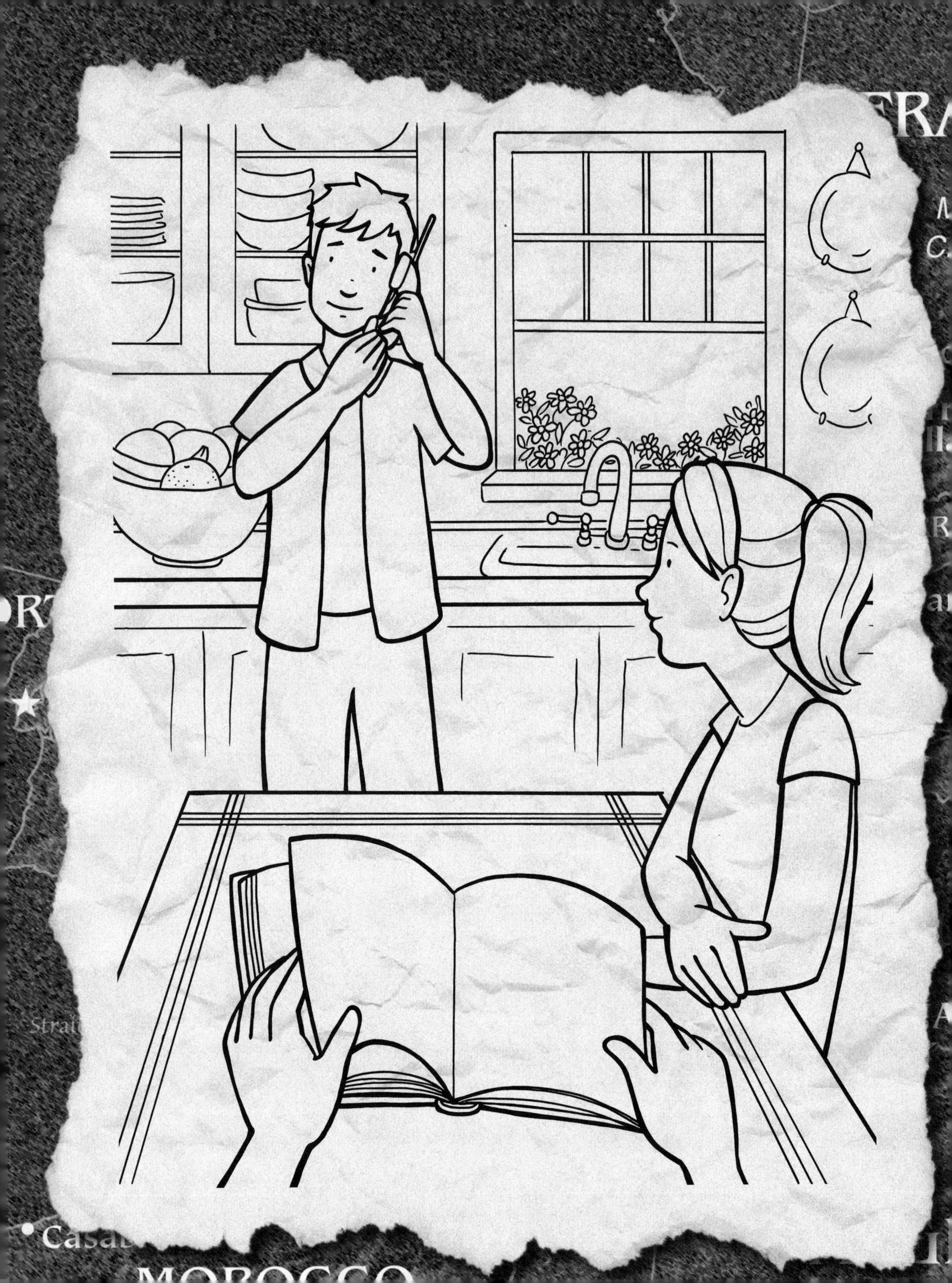
MOROCCO

The Rest of the Clue

SECTION 1.3.2 • THE REST OF THE CLUE

Lisa, Tony, y *tú* sit down to a late *cena* that *la Señora Panadero* warms up for you. You've just finished eating and are starting to puzzle over your new clue when *la inspectora Gutierrez* walks in slowly.

"We wondered *dónde* you were!" *exclama* Lisa. "We went to the *policía* station to report on *las personas* in that black van, but nobody had seen you."

"That's odd," *dice la inspectora* tiredly. "No one told me. So, *¿qué* did you learn from *el Profesor Alvarez?*"

"He gave us this," *responde* Tony, handing her the clue. "We were trying to figure it out."

Just then, *el teléfono* rings. *La Señora Panadero* answers, then hands *el teléfono* to Tony. Tony listens intently, then says, "*Sí, entiendo. Muchas gracias. Hasta luego.*" He hangs up *el teléfono*. "That was *Profesor Alvarez,*" he explains to you. "He forgot to tell us *una cosa*. The estate of *el tercer caballero* has been turned into a shelter for abandoned *animales.*"

"*¡Fantástico!*" *exclamas*. "Did he tell you *dónde la llave* is hidden?"

"No, we have to figure that out on our own," *responde* Tony.

"*Bueno,*" *dice la inspectora*. "I'll take you there *en la mañana*. For now, though, let's all get some rest." With that, *la inspectora* heads upstairs.

"Does anyone else think *la inspectora Gutierrez* was acting weird?" Lisa whispers.

"She seemed tired, or maybe sad," *respondes*.

"I don't think she's telling us everything," Tony whispers. "Remember, we spent half the afternoon in her *oficina* and never saw her. We'd better be more careful."

You thumb through Grandpa Glen's travel journal, looking for something else to help you find *la tercera llave*, when you come across a strange drawing. The words "*los huevos de oro*" are written beside the number three around an oval shape in a tree.

"What does *los huevos de oro* mean?" Lisa asks.

In this section you will:

- Practice your translation skills.
- Learn a Spanish saying and two new phrases.
- Learn about foods in different Spanish-speaking countries.
- Master meal-related vocabulary in Spanish.
- Increase your Spanish vocabulary and storytelling skills with this DiglotWeave™ story.
- Learn the phrases and grammar you would need to plan a trip to a farm.
- Improve your reading and listening comprehension skills and increase your Spanish vocabulary using a passage describing Mario's farm.
- Improve your Spanish grammar by learning about the past tense of regular Spanish verbs.

(continued)

Disc 3   Track 7

In this section you will:

→ Write a postcard to practice what you have learned.

→ Learn about the Mexican holiday *Cinco de Mayo*.

→ Develop your Spanish writing skills by writing about some of the holidays you celebrate.

→ Hone your Spanish grammar skills by learning more about Spanish past tense.

→ Solidify what you have learned about phone conversations, telling time, past tense verbs, and foods.

"*No sé,*" *respondes,* "*pero* I think we'd better try to work it out on our own. I'm not tired yet. Let's get in some studying before we go to sleep."

To solve this new clue, you'll need to learn about foods and animals, and you'll need to start learning a new story.

Journal

ACTIVITY 46

INSTRUCTIONS ¡Buenos días! Listen to the following paragraph describing a typical day, then read it out loud. Write down what the underlined phrases mean in English. Check your answers in Appendix A, on page 261. ¡Es divertido!

Por la mañana, 1. *me despierto* a las siete y cuarto y yo como el cereal. Me gusta mucho el cereal. 2. *Después*, me visto en los jeans y un suéter. 3. *Yo voy* a la escuela en el autobús a las ocho y 4. *hablo* con mis amigos. Yo voy a mis clases, y después de la escuela, yo voy a mi casa. Yo como con mi familia y yo miro televisión también. A las ocho y media de la noche, 5. *me duermo*.

1. ....
2. ....
3. ....
4. ....
5. ....

In this activity you will:
- Practice your translation skills.
- Learn a Spanish saying and two new phrases.

Disc 3   Track 8

Two New Phrases

Do you wear a watch? Do you need to know what time it is? So far, you know how to use *de la mañana, de la tarde, y de la noche* to refer to the different times of day. You also know how to say the numbers 1–60 so that you can tell time. Review the numbers you already know. Then you will be ready to learn two new phrases.

What time do you eat lunch? Usually it is about 12 P.M. or *son las doce de la tarde*. An easier way to say the same thing is *mediodía*, which means "noon." Can you see how *mediodía*—*medio* (middle) and *día* (day)—means "noon" since it is in the middle of the day? The same is true for 12 A.M. or *son las doce de la mañana*. It can be said *medianoche*—midnight, the middle of the night.

Refrán

Here's another *refrán*. Practice saying it out loud several times and try to use it today in a conversation.

¡No tengas pelos en la lengua!
Literal translation: Don't have hair on your tongue!
Meaning: Speak up!

215

ACTIVITY 46 • JOURNAL POWER-GLIDE SPANISH JUNIOR I

Performance Challenge

Individual Make a list of several things you might do at noon/*mediodía*. Choose an item from your list and write a short paragraph about it.

Performance Challenge

Group Review numbers as a class. Have two students stand up and challenge each other in a race to correctly identify the Spanish word for a number that the teacher calls out. The winning student will challenge another student while the losing student sits down.

ACTIVITY 47 • LAS MERIENDAS

Las meriendas

How many times do you eat every day? Most people eat *el desayuno* (breakfast), *el almuerzo* (lunch), and *la cena* (dinner), plus *las meriendas o los bocadillos* (snacks) in between each meal.

INSTRUCTIONS Here are several snacks. Listen to and repeat the new words.

- la limonada
- las quesadillas
- las papas fritas
- la leche
- la gaseosa
- el queso
- el helado
- las galletas
- las verduras
- la fruta

ACTIVITY 47

✓ **In this activity you will:**
→ Learn about foods in different Spanish-speaking countries.
→ Master meal-related vocabulary in Spanish.

Disc **3** Track **9**

Bananas and Eggs

Did you know that the Spaniards brought bananas to the Americas? Bananas have become such a popular and important food in Spanish-speaking countries that in Costa Rica coffee and bananas are the main exports. Did you know that most children in Spain don't eat eggs for breakfast but they do eat them for dinner? People in *México*, however, are known for having eggs as part of their big breakfasts.

ACTIVITY 47 • LAS MERIENDAS   POWER-GLIDE SPANISH JUNIOR I

Matching

INSTRUCTIONS   Match the following snacks with their pictures. Draw a line connecting the word and the picture. Remember to say the word out loud when matching them. It's good practice! Check your answers in Appendix A, on page 261.

4. las galletas
2. las papas fritas
3. la leche
5. las quesadillas
1. el queso

Eating Customs

Eating and drinking customs are different all over the world and even within each country. In some markets in *México*, they sell soda pop in glass bottles. In order to keep glass bottles off the streets and sidewalks, which could get broken and hurt people, soda pop is also sold in plastic bags! People are encouraged to drink soda pop with a straw from a plastic bag. Drinking from a bag with a straw is definitely an adventure. You need to remember that you can't set your bag down or it will roll to the side and spill all of your soda pop. Also, once your straw hits the bottom of your bag you need to carefully move it around or you will start sucking your bag up instead of the pop. Try drinking soda pop from a bag. All you need is a straw, a bag (small sandwich bags work well), and some soda pop. Remember to hold your bag carefully as you pour and don't set it down until you are done drinking. Have fun! Also, remember that like all other things you have learned, just because some people in *México* drink soda pop from a bag doesn't mean that everyone in *México* does.

Did you know that in some Spanish-speaking countries lunch can be eaten as late as 3 P.M.? Then a snack (*una merienda*) is served as late as 5–6 P.M. and a light dinner (*la cena*) between 9–10 P.M.

Sweetened breads and pastries are excellent and very popular in Spanish-speaking countries. You can go to a *panadería* or a *pastelería* to find some wonderful baked goods. Have you ever tried a *churro*? You may have tasted a *churro* in one of the many Mexican restaurants in the United States.

Churros

A *churro* is dough that is deep-fried and rolled in sugar and cinnamon. *Churros* can be made quickly and they taste great! Try some! Be sure to have your parents help you make the *churros* since it requires deep frying in hot oil.

Ingredients
- Vegetable or Olive Oil
- 1 cup water
- 1/2 cup margarine or butter
- 1/4 teaspoon salt
- 1 cup all-purpose flour
- 3 eggs
- 1/4 cup sugar
- 1/4 teaspoon ground cinnamon (optional)

Directions

Prepare to fry the *churros* by heating oil in a pan (1 to 1 1/2 inches) to 360 degrees F.

To make *churro* dough, heat water, margarine and salt to rolling boil in 3-quart saucepan; stir in flour. Stir vigorously over low heat until mixture forms a ball, about 1 minute; remove from heat. Beat eggs all at once; continue beating until smooth and then add to saucepan while stirring mixture.

Spoon mixture into cake decorator's tube with large star tip (like the kind used to decorate cakes). Squeeze 4-inch strips of dough into hot oil. Fry 3 or 4 strips at a time until golden brown, turning once, about 2 minutes on each side. Drain on paper towels. Mix sugar and the optional cinnamon and roll the *churros* in the mixture. Enjoy!

Do you usually drink juice for breakfast? In Spain children drink juice *(el zumo)* for breakfast but it is almost as common to see children drinking coffee with their breakfast.

Juice is a completely different subject in Latin America. Children and adults drink a lot of juice or *el jugo*. *El jugo* is most often made fresh and when walking on the streets or in the market, you can usually find stands that sell *aguas frescas*. These are made from fresh fruits, water, and a little sugar. They may sell juice made from watermelon, strawberry, melon, rice, etc. Yes, rice! These drinks are cool and refreshing and very popular.

There are more than 1,000 different kinds of chiles (hot peppers) and they come in all different sizes, shapes, and flavors! In some Latin American countries, people love to eat hot peppers so their food is very spicy.

Do you like to eat grapes? If you eat them during the wintertime, there's a good chance they were grown in Latin America. When it is wintertime in the United States, it is summertime in Chile and Argentina, so they grow the grapes and export them to the United States. That way you can enjoy them all year!

What Do You Like to Eat?

1. What is your favorite snack to eat after school?

   ....

2. Do you have any snacks with special memories?

   ....

3. If you could choose anything to eat on a Saturday morning when you don't have to go to school what would it be? Why?

   ....

4. If you could choose a morning snack from the list of snacks you just learned about, what would it be? Why?

   ....

5. If you could pack a snack in your backpack to have on the bus ride home, what would it be?

   ....

Arroz con leche

In Spanish-speaking countries, one popular dessert or snack is rice pudding— *arroz con leche*.

Ingredients
- 1 cup cooked rice
- 2 cups milk
- 1/2 cup white sugar
- 1 Tbsp. cinnamon

Directions

Put everything together and cook over medium–low heat for about 20 minutes or until all of the milk has been absorbed by the rice. Cool and serve. Sprinkle cinnamon or cinnamon sugar over the top.

Snack Quiz

INSTRUCTIONS Circle the letter of the correct English meaning of each word. Say each of the words out loud, working on your pronunciation. Check your answers in Appendix A, on page 261.

1. *las galletas*
   - A. chicken
   - B. cookies
   - C. cheese

2. *la leche*
   - A. milk
   - B. cheese tortillas
   - C. lemonade

3. *las verduras*
   - A. french fries
   - B. vegetables
   - C. soda pop

4. *la quesadilla*
   - A. cheese
   - B. milk
   - C. cheese tortilla

5. *el helado*
   - A. ice cream
   - B. cookies
   - C. fruit

6. *la limonada*
   - A. vegetables
   - B. lime
   - C. lemonade

7. *la gaseosa*
   - A. lemonade
   - B. soda pop
   - C. milk

ACTIVITY 47 • LAS MERIENDAS

8. *las papas fritas*
   A. vegetables
   B. french fries
   C. potatoes

9. *la fruta*
   A. fruit
   B. milk
   C. juice

10. *el queso*
    A. ice cream
    B. cookies
    C. cheese

Label the Pictures

INSTRUCTIONS   Write in the correct Spanish word below each picture. Check your answers in Appendix A, on page 261.

1. _____

2. _____

3. _____

4. _____

5. _____

Performance Challenge

Individual Make a list of the various items of food and snacks that you like to eat. Write out the time of the day that you would normally eat those foods.

Performance Challenge

Group Divide the class into teams. Have one student from each team sit in a chair at the front of the classroom. The first student to stand up and translate the word called out into Spanish wins a point for their team.

Los huevos de oro

INSTRUCTIONS Listen to the following vocabulary words from the story of *Los huevos de oro*.

Vocabulary

English	Spanish
once upon a time	había una vez
a farmer	un granjero
five chickens	cinco gallinas
three geese (female)	tres gansas
two sheep	dos ovejas
one old cow	una vaca vieja
his wife	su esposa
animals	animales
one morning	una mañana
the barn	el granero
one of the geese (female)	una de las gansas
gold	oro
the egg	el huevo
a golden egg	un huevo de oro
Look!	¡Mire!
she	ella
he	él
house	casa
poor	pobre
the city	la ciudad
money	dinero

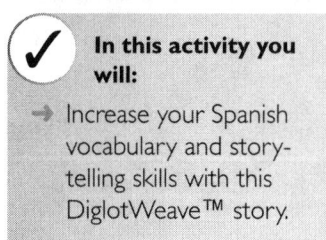

In this activity you will:

→ Increase your Spanish vocabulary and story-telling skills with this DiglotWeave™ story.

Disc **3**   Track **10**

Vocabulary (cont.)

English	Spanish
a tree	*un árbol*
farm	*granja*
a mansion	*una mansión*
ten	*diez*
more	*más*
a king	*un rey*
a wolf	*un lobo*

The Golden Eggs—*Los huevos de oro*

INSTRUCTIONS   First listen and follow along as the story is read to you. Then read the story out loud on your own to practice reading and speaking Spanish correctly. The English translation is in Appendix A, on page 261.

Había una vez, there was a farmer, *un granjero*, and his wife. They grew grain and vegetables, but they also kept a few animals: *cinco gallinas, tres gansas, dos ovejas, y una vaca vieja. El granjero y su esposa* worked hard and took care of their fields *y animales*, but they were still very poor.

Una mañana, things began to change. *La esposa del granjero* went to *el granero* to collect eggs from *las gallinas y las gansas*. She was surprised to see that *una de las gansas* had laid an egg of what looked like *oro*. *El huevo* glittered brightly in the sunlight and was very heavy. *La esposa del granjero* picked it up and dropped it onto the hard floor of *el granero*. *El huevo* didn't break! It really was *un huevo de oro*! *La esposa del granjero* ran to show her husband. "¡*Mire*! Look at this!" *ella* shouted.

El granjero was very puzzled. "Where did you get that?" *él* asked.

"*La gansa* laid it," *ella* explained. "I found it just now *en el granero*. Let's take it to the town and sell it so we can build a fine new *casa*."

El granjero shook his head. "No, I am *un granjero pobre*. If I took that much *oro* into town at once, people would wonder where I'd gotten it."

"You're right. They would come and take our *gansa*," gasped *la esposa*.

El granjero nodded solemnly. "Perhaps we should hide *el huevo* until we can go to *la ciudad* to trade it for *dinero*," *él* suggested. And so *el granjero y su esposa* hid *los huevos de oro* inside of *un árbol* near their *casa*.

The next *mañana* when *la esposa del granjero* went to *el granero*, *ella* found that *la gansa* had laid another *huevo de oro*. Even more excited than before, *ella* ran to the field where *su esposo* was working. "¡*Mire*!" she shouted. "Another one! Now we can buy a bigger *granja* as well as a nicer *casa*." Her eyes took on a greedy gleam. "With *tres huevos de oro*, we could buy the finest *granja* for miles around. With *cuatro*, we could buy *una mansión*. With *diez*, we'd be able to live like *un rey*, in a palace..." *Ella* suddenly had a great idea. "We should kill *la gansa* and get all its *huevos de oro* right now."

El granjero shook his head and said, "I think *la gansa* is fine where it is. We can wait for *más huevos*."

"But what if someone steals *la gansa*," *la esposa* worried. "Or what if *un lobo* comes at night and eats *la gansa*? We could lose all of our *huevos de oro*!"

And so that afternoon, *el granjero* killed *la gansa* only to discover that there wasn't a single *huevo de oro* inside of it. As *el granjero y su esposa* were lamenting their loss, *dos* ravens flew above them, each with a sparkling *huevo de oro* in their claws. And so, because of their greed and impatience, *el granjero y su esposa* didn't end up with any *oro* at all.

Comprehension Check

INSTRUCTIONS   Answer the following comprehension questions. Check your answers in Appendix A, on page 262.

1. What did *la esposa del granjero* find in the barn?

2. Where did *el granjero y su esposa* put the egg?

   ....

3. Were they able to get more *huevos de oro* when they killed *la gansa*?

   ....

> **Performance Challenge**
>
> *Individual* Read this segment of the story out loud and practice your Spanish pronunciation. Read the story to someone else and find out how much of the story they can understand.

> **Performance Challenge**
>
> *Group* In small groups make up an alternate ending to the story. Act out or draw a picture of the new ending.

Let's Go on a Trip!

ACTIVITY 49

Plan a trip to a farm. Mario *es un granjero y vive en la granja*. Make a list of the animals you might see while *en la granja de* Mario.

INSTRUCTIONS Match the Spanish word to the pictures to help you remember all of the animals that you already know. Draw a line connecting the word and the picture. Check your answers in Appendix A, on page 262.

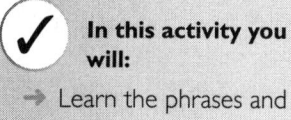

1. el pájaro
2. el caballo
3. el cerdo
4. el gato
5. la gallina
6. la vaca
7. el perro

In this activity you will:
- Learn the phrases and grammar you would need to plan a trip to a farm.

Disc **3**   Track **11**

Visiting Mario's Farm

INSTRUCTIONS Now, you need to call Mario and make plans to go to the farm. Here are a few new words to look for in this phone call. Listen to the vocabulary and then the phone conversation.

Vocabulary

English	Spanish
I want	quiero
to come	venir
they come/you all come	vienen
we'll see each other later	nos vemos

Conversation with Mario

	Spanish
•:	Bueno.
••:	¿Está Mario?
•:	Sí, es Mario.
••:	Hola Mario. Quiero venir a tu granja con mis amigos.
•:	Bueno. Mis animales son amables e interesantes. ¿Cuándo vienen a mi granja?
••:	Quiero venir por la mañana.
•:	Bien. Nos vemos mañana.
••:	Gracias y adiós Mario.

Comprehension Check

INSTRUCTIONS Answer the following comprehension questions. Check your answers in Appendix A, on page 262.

1. Who answers the phone?

   ....

2. What does Mario say about his animals?

   ....

3. When will Mario see his friend?

   ....

Trip Preparations

Sí, you are going to *la granja mañana*—tomorrow. "*Mañana*" is a word with two meanings. We already know that it means "morning" and now you have learned that it also means "tomorrow." Are you excited to go to the farm and see *los animales de* Mario? You are going to take *el coche* (car) *a la granja* and you will need some *meriendas*. *¿Qué quieres comer en el coche?* (What do you want to eat in the car?)

INSTRUCTIONS Think of 5 *meriendas* that you want to bring on your trip to the farm. Write them in Spanish and in English.

1. ....
2. ....
3. ....
4. ....
5. ....

Review of Animal Vocabulary

If Mario has *muchos animales*, where do you think they all live? What do they eat?

INSTRUCTIONS Review some of the vocabulary on animals. Listen to and repeat the following list of words.

Sentence Elements

Animals	Verbs	Adjectives	Places
la vaca	come	ruidoso	en el establo
el perro	corre	grande	en la granja
el gato	es	rápido	en la pastura
la oveja	vive	amable	
la gallina	salta	feroz	
la serpiente	ve	bajo	
el pájaro	vuela	pequeño	
el caballo	duerme		

Writing About Animals and Farms

INSTRUCTIONS Finish these few sentences about *animales*. Check your answers in Appendix A, on page 262.

1. La vaca _____ (eats) *el maíz*.
2. El gato es _____ (small).
3. La gallina _____ (lives) *en el establo*.
4. El caballo _____ (runs) *en la pastura*.
5. El perro _____ (is) *amable*.

Performance Challenge

Individual 1 What do you think *la granja de Mario* looks like? Imagine *un establo, una casa, muchos animales en la pastura, y más*. Draw a picture of *cinco* (5) things that you think will be en *la granja de Mario*.

Performance Challenge

Individual 2 Write out 5 simple sentences in *español* describing your own *granja*. What kinds of animals would you have? What would your barn look like?

1. ....
   ....
2. ....
   ....
3. ....
   ....
4. ....
   ....
5. ....
   ....

Performance Challenge

Group Have the lists of animals, verbs, adjectives, and places from the activity copied onto pieces of paper. Have small groups of students make as many sentences as they can using a set of these pieces of paper. The group that can make the most correct sentences wins.

En la granja de Mario

In this activity you will:

→ Improve your reading and listening comprehension skills and increase your Spanish vocabulary using a passage describing Mario's farm.

Disc **3** Track **12**

How exciting! *Hoy, vas a la granja de Mario a las nueve de la mañana.* Do you have your snacks? What animals will you get to see first? Maybe you will see *un establo grande y rojo con muchos animales.* Maybe you will see *los caballos en la pastura, los cerdos en la cerca,* and *las gallinas y los gatos en el establo. ¡Qué divertido!* (What fun!)

INSTRUCTIONS Describe what you think the farm may look like.

1. What will the barn look like?
   ....
2. Where will the horses be?
   ....
3. What will be inside the fence?
   ....
4. What animals will be in the barn?
   ....

Julio's Tour

INSTRUCTIONS Listen to Julio's tour of *la granja*. Read out loud to practice your Spanish. Then, get someone to read the parts with you.

Conversation at Mario's Farm

Spanish
•: *Aquí está la granja.* (Here is the farm.) *Hola Mario.*
••: *Hola.*
•: I am very excited to *ver tu granja.*

Conversation at Mario's Farm (cont.)

Spanish

●●: *Bueno. Vamos a ver a los animales. Aquí están los cerdos. Ellos son rosados y grandes. Los cerdos viven en el establo. Próximo* (next), *las gallinas y los gatos. Ellos* (they) *viven en el establo también. Afortunadamente, mi establo es muy grande y cómodo* (comfortable). *El establo es verde como* (like) *mi casa y mi garaje* (garage). *A los animales les gusta* (they like) *vivir en el establo. Detrás del establo* (behind the barn), *los caballos y las ovejas comen y corren en la pastura. La pastura es muy grande, verde, y hermosa* (beautiful).

●: *Mario, ¿te gusta* (do you like) *tener* (to have) *muchos animales?*

●●: *Sí, por supuesto* (of course). *Los animales son mis amigos y son muy amables.*

●: *Gracias por todo Mario. Vamos a mi casa pronto.*

Comprehension Check

INSTRUCTIONS Make a list of what Julio saw on *la granja de Mario* by filling in the blanks in English. Check your answers in Appendix A, on page 262.

1. The pigs are _____ and _____ .
2. The cats and the hens _____ in the barn, too.
3. The barn is very _____ and _____ .
4. The barn is _____ just like the house and the garage.
5. _____ is very big, _____ , and beautiful.
6. Does Mario like to have animals? _____
7. The animals are my _____ and they are very _____ .

Performance Challenge

Individual Draw a picture of *la granja* as Mario described it. When you are done drawing *la granja*, compare it to the picture you drew before. Write down a list of things that are the same and a list of things that are different.

My Picture

Performance Challenge

Group Have students explain to one another what they like about Mario's farm. Have students also describe what they would have on their own farm that would be different from Mario's farm.

Past Tense

ACTIVITY 51

Did you enjoy visiting Mario's farm yesterday? You will need to learn about the past tense so you can write to your family about what you did yesterday. Everything you did yesterday is in the past tense because it is something that has already happened.

INSTRUCTIONS Look at some verbs. First, each verb will appear in the present tense followed by an example of the verb being used in the present tense. Then you will read the past tense version of the same verb and an example of how the past tense verb is used.

Present Tense and Past Tense

	English	Spanish
1.	he/she/it lives	*vive*
	The horse lives in the stable.	*El caballo vive en el establo.*
2.	he/she/it lived	*vivió*
	The horse lived in the stable.	*El caballo vivió en el establo.*
3.	he/she/it runs	*corre*
	The sheep runs in the pasture.	*La oveja corre en la pastura.*
4.	he/she/it ran	*corrió*
	The sheep ran in the pasture.	*La oveja corrió en la pastura.*
5.	he/she/it is	*es*
	Mario is a farmer.	*Mario es un granjero.*
6.	he/she/it was	*fue*
	Mario was a farmer.	*Mario fue un granjero.*
7.	he/she/it eats	*come*
	The cow eats in the barn.	*La vaca come en el establo.*
8.	he/she/it ate	*comió*
	The cow ate in the barn.	*La vaca comió en el establo.*
9.	I go	*voy*
	I go to the farm.	*Yo voy a la granja.*

In this activity you will:
- Improve your Spanish grammar by learning about the past tense of regular Spanish verbs.
- Write a postcard to practice what you have learned.

Present Tense and Past Tense (cont.)

English	Spanish
10. I went	*fui*
I went to the farm.	Yo *fui a la granja.*

Using the Past Tense

Past tense is pretty simple and very helpful. Almost every story that you tell uses the past tense. You probably don't think about it much when you are speaking in your native language, but when you are learning a new language, it becomes difficult to share stories and experiences if you don't know how to use the past tense.

INSTRUCTIONS Try using a few verbs in the past tense. Fill in the blank with the correct past tense version of the verb in parentheses. Check your answers in Appendix A, on page 263.

1. La vaca _____ (ran) *rápidamente en la pastura.*
2. El cerdo _____ (lived) *en la cerca.*
3. El perro _____ (ate) *en la casa con el granjero.*
4. La gallina _____ (was) *mi amiga.*
5. El caballo _____ (ate) *el maíz.*

This time, write down what each sentence says in *inglés*. Read out loud before you translate.

6. *La oveja corrió rápidamente en la pastura.*

   ....

7. *El gato comió en el establo con las gallinas.*

   ....

8. *El perro fue al establo.*

   ....

9. *El caballo vivió en la pastura.*

   ....

Papel picado

Papel picado—paper cutting— is a traditional art from Mexico that has been around for a long time. Some *papel picado* can be very, very detailed and beautiful. *Papel picado* is used to decorate an area where a fiesta will be held. Many times *papel picado* is hung along the streets, in special rooms, and on banquet tables.

Write a Postcard

INSTRUCTIONS   Now you can use what you know about the past tense to write a quick postcard to your family. Check your answers in Appendix A, on page 263.

¡Querido _____!

Hola. Ayer (yesterday), yo 1._____ (I went) a la granja de Mario. El perro 2._____ (ran) al establo. El caballo 3._____ (ate) y 4._____ (ran) en la pastura. La oveja 5._____ (ate) mucho. El granjero 6._____ (lived) en la casa.

¡Adiós!

_____
(your Spanish name)

Performance Challenge

Individual   Make a list of the things you did yesterday. Use past tense constructions for the verbs in your list.

Performance Challenge

Group   Divide students into teams and have one student from each team come up to the chalkboard. The first student to correctly write out the past tense form of the word the teacher calls out wins a point for their team.

Cinco de Mayo

ACTIVITY 52

In this activity you will:
- Learn about the Mexican holiday *Cinco de Mayo*.
- Develop your Spanish writing skills by writing about some of the holidays you celebrate.

"Cinco de Mayo" is a celebration and is named after a date. Can you guess when it is celebrated? Look at the name *"Cinco de Mayo."* If you said May 5th, you are correct. *Cinco* means 5 and *Mayo* means May, as in the month of May. *¡Bien hecho!* (Well done!)

Many people are confused and think that *Cinco de Mayo* is Mexico's Independence Day. Actually, *Cinco de Mayo* commemorates a different but very important event. On May 5, 1862, an army of about 4,000 Mexicans took on and defeated a French army twice their size in the battle of Puebla. This small, Mexican army was victorious in just one battle, not a whole war, but the courage, commitment, and bravery shown by this much smaller army is an event that many Mexicans talk about and celebrate with great pride.

Cinco de Mayo celebrations vary a great deal. There are parades, fireworks, special programs, music, speeches, and always a lot of great food! *Cinco de Mayo* is a Mexican holiday that is celebrated by many people in the United States. There are many cities and towns with large populations of Mexicans that celebrate *Cinco de Mayo* with parades, food, and many other festivities.

You have learned a little bit about *Cinco de Mayo*. Visit <http://www.power-glide.com/go/?key=cinco-de-mayo> to learn more about *Cinco de Mayo*. As you connect to the different links, you will find photos, stories, history, recipes, and much more. Check them out! You can also look up *"Cinco de Mayo"* in the encyclopedia or on the internet. There are many books written about *Cinco de Mayo* so you might want to visit the library and check some out. Have fun!

What is Your Favorite Holiday?

INSTRUCTIONS Make a list of a few holidays that you, your family, and your community celebrate. (Holidays often come from religious activities or groups, different cultures, and political/country events.)

1. ....
2. ....
3. ....
4. ....
5. ....

What is your favorite holiday? How do you celebrate it and why is it your favorite?

....

....

....

....

....

....

....

Do you celebrate a holiday that is similar in any way to *Cinco de Mayo*? Describe it.

....

....

....

....

....

....

....

....

....

....

....

Make a *piñata*

You will need

Newspaper
Balloon
Flour
Water
Paints
Bright colored tissue paper
Old clothes (You will probably get messy. Make sure to lay down newspaper.)

1. Put air into the balloon. Decide what you are going to make. You may use several balloons to make different parts of any creature or object. You may also use some light cardboard to make legs, arms, etc.

2. Tear the newspaper into long, strips about 1 1/2–2 inches wide. Make a paste from the flour and water. Keep adding flour until your paste is about like pancake mix.

3. Dip your newspaper into the paste and then squeeze off the extra paste. You want your paper damp with the paste but don't leave any extra globs or liquid on the newspaper strip.

4. Start papering your creature. Do one strip at a time and smooth it on with your fingers. Make sure to get the excess paste off.

5. Do one even layer and then let it dry at least overnight and maybe longer. Wait until it is totally dry before you add the next layer.

6. You may need to add 3–4 layers but don't make it too tough or no one will be able to break it!

7. When the last layer on the piñata is dry, you can start decorating it. Use paint, tissue paper, etc. and have a great time!

8. Cut a hole and insert your candies and treats. Save the piece you cut out to seal the hole when you are done filling it.

Performance Challenge

Individual 1 Create your own holiday. Decide what you are celebrating, why it's important, how you want to celebrate it, when you want to celebrate it, and where you will hold the celebration. Talk about food, decorations, music, a parade, etc.

Make *papel picado*

You will need

Bright colored tissue paper

Scissors

String or yarn

Glue or tape

1. Fold your tissue paper in half, then half again. Keep folding until it is as small as you want it to be. The folding is similar to making a paper snowflake.

2. Use your scissors to cut a design. Remember not to cut all the way through a fold. You can cut random designs or you can make a specific design. (Ex. People, animals, buildings, flowers, etc.)

3. Stretch string or yarn around the room or table, then glue or tape all the pieces of *papel picado* to the string. Remember to hang the string high enough that the *papel picado* doesn't get wrecked when people are walking around the room.

4. Enjoy the beauty! You may want to leave the *papel picado* up long after your *fiesta!*

Performance Challenge

Individual 2 Make some decorations for a *fiesta*. Look at the instructions in this activity for how to make some *papel picado* or a *piñata*.

Performance Challenge

Group Have students research more about *Cinco de Mayo* in small groups. Have each small group share with the class some of the interesting things they find out.

More Past Tense

Here are a few more present and past tense verbs for you to learn and use. The more you know, the more you can communicate!

INSTRUCTIONS First you will see a present tense verb and an example of how that verb is used. Then you will see that same verb in the past tense followed by a similar example showing how it is used in a sentence.

More Present and Past Tense

English	Spanish
1. he/she talks	*habla*
Carlos talks to Maria.	*Carlos habla a María.*
2. he/she talked	*habló*
Carlos talked to Maria.	*Carlos habló a María.*
3. he/she sleeps	*duerme*
The horse sleeps in the barn.	*El caballo duerme en el establo.*
4. he/she slept	*durmió*
The horse slept in the barn.	*El caballo durmió en el establo.*
5. he/she says	*dice*
The farmer says, "Hi."	*El granjero dice, "Hola."*
6. he/she said	*dijo*
The farmer said, "Hi."	*El granjero dijo, "Hola."*
7. he/she/it flies	*vuela*
The bird flies a lot.	*El pájaro vuela mucho.*
8. he/she/it flew	*voló*
The bird flew a lot.	*El pájaro voló mucho.*
9. he/she/it sees	*ve*
The cow sees the farm.	*La vaca ve la granja.*
10. he/she/it saw	*vio*
The cow saw the farm.	*La vaca vio la granja.*

ACTIVITY 53

✓ **In this activity you will:**

→ Hone your Spanish grammar skills by learning more about Spanish past tense.

Piñatas

La piñata is one of the most popular decorations and activities at most fiestas in Spanish-speaking countries. *Piñatas* are made of clay or *papiermache* and are usually shaped like animals. Candy, fruit, and toys fill the inside of a piñata. Sometimes one special item is included in the *piñata* and whoever finds that item is supposed to have good luck. *Piñatas* are hung up in the air from a tree, the ceiling, or anything high and sturdy. Children or adults are blindfolded, given a stick, and spun around to make sure they don't know where the piñata is. Then they swing at the *piñata* and try to break it. When the piñata breaks, all the treats fall, and everyone rushes in to get them.

More Present and Past Tense (cont.)

	English	Spanish
11.	I see.	*veo*
	I see the animals.	Yo *veo* a los animales.
12.	I saw	*vi*
	I saw the animals.	Yo *vi* a los animales.

Performance Challenge

Individual Write a short story in Spanish in the past tense. Use any of the Spanish words that you already know. Fill in the words that you don't know in Spanish with English. Share your story with someone.

Performance Challenge

Group Write a story in small groups using the past tense verbs found in this activity. Each group should be able to share their story with the rest of the class.

Repaso

ACTIVITY 54

Review what you have learned about phone conversations, telling time, past tense verbs, and snacks. Look how much you know!

A Phone Conversation

INSTRUCTIONS Listen to this phone conversation and figure out what these two people are talking about.

Carlos Calls Miguel

Spanish
•: Aló.
••: Buenos días. ¿Está Miguel? Yo quiero hablar con Miguel.
•: Sí, un momento.
••: Hola. Es Miguel. ¿Quién habla?
•: Es Carlos. ¿Querrías ir a la granja mañana?
••: Sí, por supuesto. Me gustan los animales mucho. Mi animal favorito es el cerdo.
•: Bueno. Me gustan los animales también.
••: ¿A qué hora querrías ir a la granja?
•: Yo quiero ir a las dos de la tarde.
••: Nos vemos mañana a las dos de la tarde.
•: Adiós.

In this activity you will:
→ Solidify what you have learned about phone conversations, telling time, past tense verbs, and foods.

Disc **3** Track **13**

Now read through this phone conversation with a friend, classmate, teacher, or family member. If they don't know Spanish, this will be a great chance for you to teach them. Try switching parts. Have fun!

Comprehension Check

INSTRUCTIONS Look back over the phone conversation and answer the following questions. Check your answers in Appendix A, on page 263.

1. Who was calling Miguel?

   ....

2. Where does Carlos want to go?

   ....

3. Do they both like animals?

   ....

4. What time are they going to the farm?

   ....

Telling Time

INSTRUCTIONS When you are making plans, you will need to be able to tell time. Review a little bit about telling time. Circle the letter of the correct English translation of these phrases. Check your answers in Appendix A, on page 263.

1. *Y media*
   - A. and the middle
   - B. half an hour, 30 minutes after
   - C. in the morning (A.M.)

2. *Medianoche*
   - A. midnight
   - B. afternoon
   - C. early morning

3. *Y cuarto*
   - A. half an hour, 30 minutes after
   - B. quarter to the hour, 15 minutes before the hour
   - C. quarter past the hour, 15 minutes after the hour

4. *Son las...*
   - A. it is...
   - B. are the...
   - C. half an hour, 30 minutes after

5. *De la mañana*
   A. in the morning (A.M.)
   B. in the evening (P.M.)
   C. sometime tomorrow

6. *¿Qué hora es?*
   A. When is it?
   B. What is it?
   C. What time is it?

7. *De la noche*
   A. in the evening (P.M.)
   B. half an hour, 30 minutes after
   C. in the morning (A.M.)

8. *Menos cuarto*
   A. minus a minute
   B. quarter past the hour, 15 minutes after the hour
   C. quarter to the hour, 15 minutes before the hour

¿Qué hora es?

INSTRUCTIONS Write in the time. Check your answers in Appendix A, on page 263.

ex. *Son las tres y veinte.* 3:20

1. *Son las once menos cuarto.* _____
2. *Son las ocho y media.* _____
3. *Son las siete y diecinueve.* _____
4. *Son las dos y cuarto.* _____
5. *Son las cinco y cincuenta y dos.* _____

Reading Comprehension

INSTRUCTIONS Read the story out loud on your own and then answer the questions. Check your answers in Appendix A, on page 263.

Ayer, yo fui a la granja en mi coche con Marta. Marta comió la fruta y las galletas en el coche. Ella comió mucha fruta. En la granja, el gato dijo, "Miau!" y en la pastura la vaca dijo, "Muu!" Mario, el granjero, habló a Marta. Yo vi a los caballos en la pastura también. Marta vio a unas ovejas blancas.

1. Where did Marta go?
   ....

2. What *meriendas* (snacks) did Marta eat?
   ....

3. Which animals made noise?
   ....

4. Who talked to Marta at the farm?
   ....

5. What did Marta see?
   ....

Performance Challenge

Individual   Play a memory game with Power-Glide Flash Cards or make your own flash cards. Try to match up all the vocabulary words and phrases to their correct meanings.

Performance Challenge

Group   Divide the class into teams and have students go up to the chalkboard. Ask a combination of questions from this activity as well as other activities and let students race to answer them correctly to win a point for their team.

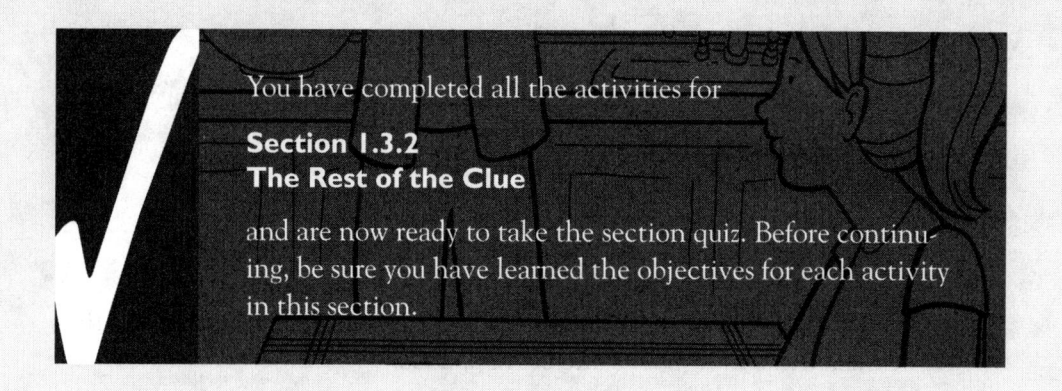

SECTION 1.3.2 • THE REST OF THE CLUE

> You have completed all the activities for
> **Section 1.3.2**
> **The Rest of the Clue**
> and are now ready to take the section quiz. Before continuing, be sure you have learned the objectives for each activity in this section.

Section 1.3.2 Quiz

Disc **3**   Track **14**

INSTRUCTIONS First, review with your flash cards to get warmed up and to refresh your Spanish memory. Second, listen to this paragraph and answer the questions. Third, read the paragraph on your own and finish answering the questions. Make sure you read the questions before you start listening. Check your answers in Appendix A, on page 264.

Mario Talks About His Farm

Spanish
•: Aquí está la granja. Hola Mario.
••: Hola.
•: We are very excited to *ver tu granja*.
••: Bueno. Vamos a ver a los animales. Aquí están los cerdos. Ellos son rosados y grandes. Los cerdos viven en el establo. Próximo, las gallinas y los gatos. Ellos viven en el establo también. Afortunadamente, mi establo es muy grande y cómodo. El establo es verde como mi casa y mi garaje. A los animales les gusta vivir en el establo. Detrás del establo, los caballos y las ovejas comen y corren en la pastura. La pastura es muy grande, verde, y hermosa.

1. **What color are the pigs?**

   ....

2. **Where do the pigs live?**

   ....

3. **Is the barn big?**

   ....

4. Where do the horses and the sheep eat and run?

....

5. What is the pasture like?

....
....

INSTRUCTIONS Fill in the blanks with the past tense form of the verb in parentheses. Remember, these things have already happened.

6. Yo _____ (went) *a la granja ayer.*

7. *El caballo* _____ (went) *al establo.*

8. *El cerdo* _____ (lived) *en el establo.*

9. *La vaca* _____ (ate) *en la pastura con la oveja.*

10. *Mario* _____ (talked) *a los animales mucho.*

....

INSTRUCTIONS Circle the letter of the correct English definition for the past tense Spanish verb.

11. *fue*
    A. he/she was
    B. he/she flew
    C. he/she came

12. *vivió*
    A. he/she ate
    B. he/she said
    C. he/she lived

13. *comió*
    A. he/she was
    B. he/she came
    C. he/she ate

14. *habló*
    A. he/she talked
    B. he/she said
    C. he/she had

15. *dijo*
    A. he/she said
    B. he/she talked
    C. he/she did

INSTRUCTIONS Fill in the blanks to tell the time.

16. **8:40 A.M.**
    Son las _____ y _____ de la _____.

17. **10:15 P.M.**
    Son las diez y _____ de la _____.

18. **9:30 A.M.**
    Son las _____ y _____ de la _____.

19. **2:45 P.M.**
    Son las tres menos _____ de la _____.

20. **4:20 P.M.**
    Son las cuatro y _____ de la _____.

¡Muy bien hecho!

✓ You have completed all the sections for
Module 1.3
Be sure you have learned the objectives for each activity in this module.

✓ You have completed all the modules for
Junior 1
Congratulations for completing Power-Glide Spanish Junior 1. Use Spanish every day and become a lifelong learner.

Appendix A
Student Answer Keys

Answers to activity questions and exercises are provided for checking the student's own work.

Activity Answers

Activity 2: *Las naciones*

Puerto Rico, Cuba,
Spain, Mexico,
Dominican Republic,
Honduras and Belize,
Guatemala,
Nicaragua, Costa Rica,
Panama, Colombia,
Venezuela,

Ecuador, El Salvador,
Bolivia, Peru,
Chile and Paraguay,
And Uruguay also,
Argentina, and so
We remember the Latin American countries.

Activity 3: Greetings Quiz

1. B
2. B
3. A
4. C
5. B
6. C

Activity 4: Translating Exercise

1. there is/there are
2. big/large
3. rapidly/quickly
4. much/a lot
5. the zoo
6. favorite
7. but

Activity 6: Self Quiz

1. B
2. C
3. A
4. B
5. A
6. C
7. A
8. B

Activity 7: Adjectives

1. The lion is big and ferocious.
2. The cow is nice and black.
3. My pig is noisy and pink.
4. The horse is tall and fast.

Activity 7: Create Your Own Sentences

1. *La gallina es amable y café/marrón.*
2. *El perro es café/marrón y grande.*
3. *El pájaro es ruidoso y pequeño.*
4. *El tigre es anaranjado y negro.*

Activity 7: Draw and Describe

1. The lion is yellow and ferocious.
2. The elephant is gray and big.
3. The horse is fast and tall.

Activity 8: The Little Red Hen—*La gallinita roja*: Part I

Once upon a time, there was a little red hen. She lived in the barnyard with the other chickens and roosters and ducks and geese. One day, this little red hen found a few grains of wheat. She decided that, instead of eating them, she would plant them.

"Who will help me plant the wheat?" she asked.

"Not I," said the rooster.

"Not I," said the duck.

"Not I," said the goose.

"Very well," said the little red hen, "I will do it myself."

And so the little red hen dug a little trench in the dirt with her beak and carefully planted each grain of wheat. She covered the seeds and stamped the dirt down just so. She gave them a little water every day. Soon her seeds grew into little green sprouts. She kept watering them and made sure her sprouts got plenty of sunlight. Before long, they grew into fine, tall wheat plants.

The plants got heavy ears of wheat on them that gradually turned ripe and golden. The rest of the wheat plants dried and turned a pale golden yellow, too. Finally, one day, the little red hen decided it was time to harvest her wheat.

"Who will help me harvest the wheat?" she asked.

"Not I," said the rooster.

"Not I," said the duck.

"Not I," said the goose.

"Very well," said the little red hen, "I will do it myself."

And so the little red hen cut down her fine, tall wheat plants and cut off the ripe heads of grain. Then it was time to thresh the wheat, to separate the good, edible parts from the tough, prickly parts.

"Who will help me thresh the wheat?" asked the little red hen.

"Not I," said the rooster.

"Not I," said the duck.

"Not I," said the goose.

"Very well," said the little red hen, "I will do it myself."

And so the little red hen threshed her wheat until she had a little bag full of plump, golden grains of wheat. The little red hen decided she wanted to make bread with it, so she needed to take it to the mill to grind it into flour.

"Who will help me grind the wheat?" asked the little red hen.

"Not I," said the rooster.

"Not I," said the duck.

"Not I," said the goose.

"Very well," said the little red hen, "I will do it myself."

And so the little red hen carried her bag of wheat to the mill, where she ground it into flour. She brought her bag of flour back home. After waiting all year, it was finally time to make bread.

Activity 8: Comprehension Check

1. Wheat.
2. No.
3. Bread.

Activity 10: Comprehension Check

1. in the jungle
2. *el tigre*
3. very well
4. runs

Activity 10: Self Quiz

1. cat

2. horse
3. chicken/hen
4. cow
5. dog
6. B
7. B
8. C
9. A
10. C
11. (a sentence containing a Spanish adjective)
12. (a sentence containing a Spanish adjective)
13. (a sentence containing a Spanish adjective)
14. (a sentence containing a Spanish adjective)
15. (a sentence containing a Spanish adjective)

Activity 11: *En la granja*

In the country, there is a large farm.
On the farm, there is a nice dog,
And the dog likes to play
With his good friends.
On the farm, there is a nice dog.

In the country, there is a large farm.
On the farm, there is a very quick cat,
And the cat chases
The rats and the chickens.
On the farm, there is a very quick cat.

In the country, there is a large farm.
On the farm, there is a fat pig, yes.
And the pig eats all that
The farmer brings.
On the farm, there is a fat pig, yes.

In the country, there is a large farm.
On the farm, there is a sheep, yes.
The sheep calmly stays
In the meadow always.
On the farm, there is a sheep, yes.

In the country, there is a large farm.
On the farm, there is a strong horse.
The horse always helps the
Farmer with everything.
On the farm, there is a strong horse.

In the country, there is a large farm.
On the farm, there is a good farmer.
The farmer takes care of all
The animals of the farm.
On the farm, there is a good farmer.

Activity 11: Comprehension Check

1. large
2. to play
3. the horse

Activity 12: Match and Learn

1. sees (picture of an eye with an arrow)
2. escapes (pictures of a box with an arrow)
3. corn
4. sleeps (picture of boy with Zs)
5. water (picture of a water faucet)
6. barn
7. fence

Activity 13: The Little Red Hen—*La gallinita roja*: Part II

"Who will help me make the bread?" asked the little red hen.

"Not I," said the rooster.

"Not I," said the duck.

"Not I," said the goose.

"Very well," said the little red hen, "I will do it myself."

And so she added and pounded and mixed and kneaded. Then she let the bread dough rise. While it was rising, she decided she should heat up the oven to bake the bread.

"Who will help me bake the bread?" asked the little red hen.

"Not I," said the rooster.

"Not I," said the duck.

"Not I," said the goose.

"Very well," said the little red hen, "I will do it myself."

So she lit a fire in the big, old-fashioned oven and carefully fed it and fanned it until she had a nice, hot bed of coals. Then she put her loaf of bread in the oven and let it bake. Mm-mmm, it smelled wonderful! Soon, the bread was done, and the little red hen took it out of the oven.

"Now," said the little red hen, "who will help me eat the bread?"

"I will," said the rooster.

"I will," said the duck.

"I will," said the goose.

"I don't think so," said the little red hen. "Did you help me plant the wheat?"

"No," said the rooster.

"No," said the duck.

"No," said the goose.

"Did you help me care for the wheat?" asked the little red hen.

"No," said the rooster.

"No," said the duck.

"No," said the goose.

"Did you help me harvest the wheat?" asked the little red hen.

"No," said the rooster.

"No," said the duck.

"No," said the goose.

"Did you help me thresh the wheat?" asked the little red hen.

"No," said the rooster.

"No," said the duck.

"No," said the goose.

Activity 13: Comprehension Check

1. No one.
2. Big.
3. The rooster, the duck, and the goose.

Activity 14: Present Tense

1. The horse lives in the barn.
2. The dog says, "woof, woof."
3. The chicken runs in the pasture.
4. The snake is very big/large.
5. The pig eats corn.

Activity 15: Comprehension Check 1

1. on the farm/in the barn
2. the pasture
3. corn
4. the barn
5. yes

Activity 15: Match and Learn

1. D
2. D
3. A
4. C
5. D
6. A
7. A
8. B
9. B
10. C
11. A

Activity 15: Comprehension Check 2

1. a friend/a farmer
2. the horse
3. the barn
4. brown
5. the animals

Activity 17: *Diez perritos*

One, two, three puppies,
Four, five, six puppies,
Seven, eight, nine puppies,
Ten puppies play.

Ten, nine, eight puppies,
Seven, six, five puppies,
Four, three, two puppies,
One puppy plays.

Activity 17: Comprehension Check

1. ten
2. five
3. eight

Activity 17: Match and Learn

1. B
2. C
3. C
4. C
5. D
6. C
7. D
8. B

Activity 19: Chores

The farmer gives hay and corn to the animals every day. The farmer watches the animals and cleans the barn and mows the pasture. The farmer is very busy. The farmer works every day. At night, the farmer sleeps in the house.

Activity 19: Comprehension Check

1. every day
2. the barn
3. yes, very busy
4. every day

Activity 20: Translation Matching

1. C
2. B
3. B
4. A
5. C
6. B
7. C
8. A

Activity 21: "Catch" the Meaning

1. the office
2. the secretary
3. bread
4. the classroom
5. listening to the radio in the barn

Activity 22: Comprehension Check

1. yes
2. reading books and magazines
3. no, it is very calm
4. the newspapers
5. silence

Activity 22: *La clase*

1. students
2. difficult
3. interesting
4. repeats
5. information

Activity 24: The Little Red Hen—*La gallinita roja*: Part III

"Did you help me grind the wheat?" asked the little red hen.

"No," said the rooster.

"No," said the duck.

"No," said the goose.

"Did you help me make the bread?" asked the little red hen.

"No," said the rooster.

"No," said the duck.

"No," said the goose.

"Did you help me bake the bread?" asked the little red hen.

"No," said the rooster.

"No," said the duck.

"No," said the goose.

"Well then," said the little red hen, "you didn't help me plant the wheat. You didn't help me care for the wheat. You didn't help me harvest the wheat. You didn't help me thresh the wheat. You didn't help me grind the wheat. You didn't help me make the bread, and you didn't help me bake the bread. Do you think you have any right to eat the bread?"

The other animals hung their heads in shame.

"No," said the rooster.

"No," said the duck.

"No," said the goose.

"That's right," said the little red hen, "you don't. But just this once, I'll be nice and share."

And so all the animals ate the fresh, delicious bread together. The next day, the goose found some more grains of wheat lying in the dirt.

"Hey, look what I found!" she called.

All the animals came over and helped her collect the wheat, and then all of them planted the wheat together.

Activity 24: Comprehension Check

1. No.
2. No. She decided to share with the rooster, the duck, and the goose.
3. They all collected and planted wheat.

Activity 25: Workers and Workplaces

1. *el correo*
2. *el restaurante*
3. *el supermercado*
4. *la biblioteca*
5. *la panadería*
6. *el cuerpo de bomberos*
7. *el banco*
8. *la granja*
9. *la escuela*
10. *la comisaría*

Activity 25: Translating Descriptions

1. The mailman carries letters to houses.
2. The banker works with a lot of money.
3. The policeman talks with the children.
4. The teacher listens to the students.
5. The farmer walks in the pasture with the animals.

Activity 25: Identify the Word

1. *el maestro*
2. *la comisaría*
3. *habla/trabaja*
4. *dice*
5. *el camarero*

Activity 25: Listening Practice

1. *trabajos*
2. *la panadería*
3. *mira*
4. *el pan*
5. *es*

Activity 26: Comprehension Check

1. a restaurant
2. "La Casa de Carlos" (Carlos' House)
3. chicken and potatoes, and enchiladas and rice
4. the waiter

Activity 28: Describing Pictures

1. El tendero dice, "Hola. ¿Puedo ayudarle?
2. El granjero trabaja con los animales en la granja.
3. La banquera trabaja en el banco.
4. El maestro habla a los estudiantes.
5. El bombero trabaja en el cuerpo de bomberos.

Activity 28: Match and Learn

1. A
2. D
3. B
4. C
5. C
6. A

Activity 29: Self Quiz

1. B
2. A
3. B
4. C
5. A
6. C
7. C
8. A
9. B
10. A
11. B
12. C
13. C
14. A

Activity 30: A.M. and P.M.

1. Son las once menos cuarto de la mañana.
2. Son las dos y media de la tarde.
3. Son las ocho y veinte y cinco de la noche.
4. Son las cuatro y cuarto de la tarde.
5. Son las siete y diez de la mañana.
6. Son las seis y diez y ocho de la mañana.
7. Son las once y treinta y ocho de la noche.

Activity 31: Comprehension Check

1. Carlos
2. Very well.
3. Go to the cafeteria to eat.
4. at 12:30 P.M.

Activity 32: Comprehension Check I

1. He is a journalist for the newspaper.
2. at the bakery
3. 5:00 A.M.
4. Because it is interesting and fun, and also because he likes to eat bread.

Activity 32: Comprehension Check II

1. dogs, horses, a cow, and sheep
2. eight sheep
3. in the pasture
4. dogs

Activity 33: The Ugly Duckling—El patito feo: parte I

Once upon a time down on an old farm, lived a duck family. Mother Duck had been sitting on a nest of new eggs for quite some time. One nice morning, the eggs hatched and out popped six little yellow ducklings. One egg was bigger than the rest, and it didn't hatch. Mother Duck couldn't recall laying that large seventh egg. How did it get there? "Tock! Tock!" The little prisoner was pecking inside his egg trying to get out like the others had done.

"Did I not count right?" Mother Duck wondered. But before she had time to think about it, the last egg finally hatched. A strange looking duckling with gray feathers gazed up at a worried mother.

The ducklings grew quickly, but Mother Duck had a secret worry. "I can't understand how this ugly duckling can be one of mine!" she said to herself. The gray duckling didn't look like the other children and he certainly wasn't pretty. He ate much more than his brothers and was quickly outgrowing them.

As the days went by, the poor ugly duckling became more and more unhappy. His brothers didn't want to play with him, he was so clumsy, and everyone at the farm laughed at him. He felt sad and lonely. Mother Duck did her best to console the poor ugly duckling. "Poor little, ugly duckling!" she would say. "Why are you so different from the others?" The ugly duckling secretly cried at night because he was so sad. He felt like nobody wanted him. "Nobody loves me, they all tease me! Why am I so different from my brothers?"

One day, he ran away from the farm. He stopped at a pond and asked all the other birds. "Do you know of any ducklings with gray feathers like mine?" But everyone shook their heads in scorn.

"We don't know anyone as ugly as you." The ugly duckling did not lose heart and went to another pond, where a pair of large geese gave him the same answer to his question. They also warned him, "Don't stay here! Go away! It's dangerous! There are men with guns around here!" The duckling was sorry he had ever left the farm. He was scared and so alone, but kept going.

His travels took him near an old cottage. The old woman who lived in the cottage caught him, thinking he was a stray goose. "I'll put you in the chicken coop so you can lay plenty of eggs for me," said the old woman whose eyesight was bad. But the ugly duckling didn't lay a single egg for the old woman. The chickens in the chicken coop didn't like having the ugly duckling around invading their space, so they tried to scare him away. "If you don't lay eggs," they said "the old woman will cook you up for dinner!" The cat that prowled around the coop added, "I hope the old woman cooks you, then I can gnaw at your bones!" The poor ugly duckling was so scared that he could not sleep nor eat. He just needed to find a way to get out of there!

Activity 33: Comprehension Check

1. She was worried that the ugly duckling wasn't really one of her children.
2. He became more and more unhappy.
3. He hoped that the old woman would cook up the ugly duckling.

Activity 34: Comprehension Check

1. talking with his mom
2. to a restaurant
3. an enchilada and milk
4. a quesadilla and some french fries

Activity 34: Matching

1. B
2. E
3. F
4. D
5. A
6. C

Activity 36: *Leyendo:* Practice Your Reading Skills

Today I am going to take my dog to work. I work at a school. I am a teacher and my students are young and very smart. The students like animals a lot and they are studying animals in class.

My dog's name is Stormy. Stormy is seven years old and lives on my farm. Stormy likes to run and play with the other animals. Stormy and I walk and play often. When I ride a horse, Stormy runs too. Stormy is my favorite animal.

Stormy is going to visit my class today and I think the students are going to love him. The students can run and play with Stormy. Later, we are going to eat ice cream and drink lemonade. Stormy likes ice cream too.

Activity 37: Comprehension Check

1. Maria
2. yes
3. the bakery
4. 2:30 P.M.

Activity 37: Questions and Answers

1. Sí, voy a hablar en español.
   No, no voy a hablar en español.
2. Sí, voy a vivir en el establo.
   No, no voy a vivir en el establo.
3. Sí, voy a trabajar mucho.
   No, no voy a trabajar mucho.
4. Sí, voy a correr con los animales.
   No, no voy a correr con los animales.
5. Sí, voy a decir, "hola."
   No, no voy a decir, "hola."

Activity 38: Comprehension Check

1. 7:00 A.M.
2. she talks to her friends
3. at her house
4. eats dinner
5. watches TV

Activity 38: Writing Practice

1. in the morning
2. in the evening
3. I go
4. he/she goes
5. I eat
6. he/she plays
7. he/she gets up
8. I take a bath
9. he/she gets dressed
10. I sleep
11. he/she sleeps

Activity 38: Listening Comprehension

1. me levanto
2. de la tarde
3. se baña
4. me visto
5. come
6. juego
7. después

Activity 39: What's Happening Today?

1. A
2. C
3. A
4. B
5. A
6. C
7. B
8. B

Activity 39: Complete the Conversation

1. G
2. D
3. E
4. A
5. F

Activity 40: Recognizing Differences

1. me baño
2. se viste
3. se duerme
4. me levanto
5. se baña

Activity 41: The Ugly Duckling—*El patito feo: parte II*

One night, finding the door of the chicken coop ajar, the ugly duckling escaped. Once again he was so alone, but at least he wasn't with those mean chickens and cat anymore. He went as far away from the old cottage as he could, and in the morning, he found himself in a thick bed of reeds. "If nobody wants me, I'll hide here forever." There was plenty of food and nobody around to scare the ugly duckling and so he began to feel happier, though he was lonely. One day at sunrise, he saw a group of beautiful birds flying overhead. They were white, with long slender necks, yellow beaks, and large wings.

"If only I could look like them, just for one day," said the duckling admiringly. Winter came in the reed bed froze. The poor duckling eventually had to leave his frozen home to search for food in the cold snow. He quickly became exhausted and fell to the ground. Fortunately, a farmer found him and put him in his big jacket pocket. "I'll take him home to my children. They'll look after him. Poor thing, he's frozen!" The duckling was showered with kindly care at the farmer's house. And so, the ugly duckling was able to survive the bitterly cold winter.

When finally Spring had arrived, the ugly duckling had grown so big that the farmer decided, "I'll set him free by the pond" When the duckling swam onto the pond he saw his reflection in the water. "I hardly recognize myself," he said. He really had grown up. He wasn't a duckling anymore. He wasn't ugly anymore either. As he sat there examining his reflection in the water, the birds with the large, white wings glided onto the pond. When the duckling saw them, he realized that his reflection matched theirs. He now looked just like them. He was one of their kind!

The beautiful birds swam near the duckling and said, "We are swans like you. Where have you been hiding? How come we have never met you before?" "It's a long story," replied the duckling, who really wasn't a duck at all, but a young swan. He happily made friends with his fellow swans and swam majestically with them on the pond.

One day, he heard children on the bank exclaim, "Look at that young swan! He's the most beautiful of all the swans!" The young swan almost burst with happiness because now he knew why he had been so different from the ducks he had grown up with. He was a beautiful swan!

Activity 41: Comprehension Check

1. A farmer took the duckling to his house where his children took care of the duckling.
2. He wished he could look like them for just one day.
3. that he was a beautiful swan

Activity 46: Journal

1. I get up
2. later
3. I go
4. I talk
5. I go to sleep

Activity 47: Matching

1. *el queso*—cheese
2. *las papas fritas*—french fries
3. *la leche*—milk
4. *las galletas*—cookies
5. *las quesadillas*—cheese tortilla

Activity 47: Snack Quiz

1. B
2. A
3. B
4. C
5. A
6. C
7. B
8. B
9. A
10. C

Activity 47: Label the Pictures

1. *la limonada*
2. *el helado*
3. *la gaseosa*
4. *los verduras*
5. *la fruta*

Activity 48: The Golden Eggs—*Los huevos de oro*

Once upon a time, there was a farmer and his wife. They grew grain and vegetables, but they also kept a few animals: five chickens, three geese, two sheep, and one old cow. The farmer and his wife worked hard and took care of their fields and animals, but they were still very poor.

One morning, things began to change. The farmer's wife went to the barn to collect eggs from the chickens and the geese. She was surprised to see that one of the geese had laid an egg of what looked like gold. The egg glittered brightly in the sunlight and was very heavy. The farmer's wife picked it up and dropped it onto the hard floor of the barn. The egg didn't break! It really was a golden egg! The farmer's wife ran to show her husband. "Look! Look at this!" she shouted.

The farmer was very puzzled. "Where did you get that?" he asked.

"The goose laid it," she explained. "I found it just now in the barn. Let's take it to town and sell it so we can build a fine new house."

The farmer shook his head. "No, I am a poor farmer. If I took that much gold into town at once, people would wonder where I'd gotten it."

"You're right. They would come and take our goose," gasped the wife.

The farmer nodded solemnly. "Perhaps we should hide the egg until we can go to the city to trade it in for money," he suggested. And so the farmer and his wife hid the golden eggs inside of a tree near their house.

The next morning when the farmer's wife went to the barn, she found that the goose had laid another golden egg. Even more excited than before, she ran to the field where her husband was working. "Look!" she shouted. "Another one! Now we can buy a bigger farm as well as a nicer house." Her eyes took on a greedy gleam. "With three golden eggs, we could buy the finest farm for miles around. With four, we could buy a mansion. With ten, we'd be able to live like a king, in a palace…" She suddenly had a great idea. "We should kill the goose and get all its golden eggs right now."

The farmer shook his head and said, "I think the goose is fine where it is. We can wait for more eggs."

"But what if someone steals the goose," the wife worried. "Or what if a wolf comes at night and eats the goose? We could lose all our golden eggs!"

And so that afternoon, the farmer killed the goose only to discover that there wasn't a single golden egg inside of it. As the farmer and his wife were lamenting their loss, two ravens flew above them, each with a sparkling golden egg in their claws. And so, because of their greed and impatience, the farmer and his wife didn't end up with any gold at all.

Activity 48: Comprehension Check

1. A golden egg
2. Inside of a tree near their house
3. No

Activity 49: Let's Go on a Trip!

1. *el pájaro*—bird
2. *el caballo*—horse
3. *el cerdo*—pig
4. *el gato*—cat
5. *la gallina*—hen/chicken
6. *la vaca*—cow
7. *el perro*—dog

Activity 49: Comprehension Check

1. Mario
2. they are nice and interesting
3. tomorrow

Activity 49: Writing About Animals and Farms

1. *come*
2. *pequeño*
3. *vive*
4. *corre*
5. *es*

Activity 50: Comprehension Check

1. pink, big
1. live
1. big, comfortable
1. green

1. the pasture, green
1. yes
1. friends, nice

Activity 51: Using the Past Tense

1. *corrió*
2. *vivió*
3. *comió*
4. *fue*
5. *comió*
6. The sheep ran fast in the pasture.
7. The cat ate in the barn with the chickens.
8. The dog went to the barn.
9. The horse lived in the pasture.

Activity 51: Write a Postcard

1. *fui*
2. *corrió*
3. *comió*
4. *corrió*
5. *comió*
6. *vivió*

Activity 54: Comprehension Check

1. Carlos
2. the farm
3. yes
4. 2:00 P.M.

Activity 54: Telling Time

1. B
2. A
3. C
4. A
5. A
6. C
7. A
8. C

Activity 54: ¿Qué hora es?

1. 10:45
2. 8:30
3. 7:19
4. 2:15
5. 5:52

Activity 54: Reading Comprehension

1. to the farm
2. fruit and cookies
3. the cat and the cow
4. Mario, the farmer
5. sheep

Section Quiz Answers

Section 1.1.1 Quiz

1. *Hola*
2. *estás*
3. *español*
4. *el león*
5. *es*
6. *feroz*
7. *vive*
8. *un poco*
9. *la vaca*—cow
10. *el tigre*—tiger
11. *el cerdo*—pig
12. *el elefante*—elephant
13. *el caballo*—horse
14. *el león*—lion
15. *la oveja*—sheep
16. *el pájaro*—bird
17. big/large
18. lives
19. the cow
20. gray

21. jumps

Section 1.1.2 Quiz

1. *el perro*—(adjective)
2. *la gallina*—(adjective)
3. *la vaca*—(adjective)
4. *el gato*—(adjective)
5. *el caballo*—(adjective)
6. The cow eats corn.
7. The dog is very noisy.
8. The pig says, "oink, oink."
9. The horse lives in the barn.
10. The sheep looks at the farmer.

Section 1.2.1 Quiz

1. *estás*
2. *trabajos*
3. *banquero*
4. *banqueros*
5. *banco*
6. *hay*
7. 1—*El tendero trabaja en el supermercado.*
8. 5—*El camarero trabaja en el restaurante.*
9. 4—*El maestro habla a los estudiantes en la escuela.*
10. 2—*El granjero es muy ocupado en la granja.*
11. 3—*El panadero trabaja en la panadería.*

Section 1.2.2 Quiz

1. B
2. B
3. A
4. B
5. A
6. *Bueno.*
7. *¿Está Roberto?*
8. *al restaurante*
9. *a las doce y media*
10. *Hasta luego*

11. *Julia va a vivir en México.*
12. *Yo voy a comer la fruta.*
13. *Tú vas a hablar por teléfono.*
14. *va*
15. *voy*
16. *vas*

Section 1.3.1 Quiz

1. *me levanto*
2. *(yo) como*
3. *(yo) voy*
4. *(yo) hablo*
5. *(yo) juego*
6. *(yo) como la cena*
7. *me duermo*
8. *a las nueve*
9. B
10. A
11. C
12. A
13. B
14. C
15. C
16. B
17. C
18. A

Section 1.3.2 Quiz

1. pink
2. the barn
3. yes
4. the pasture
5. very big, green, and beautiful
6. *fui*
7. *fue*
8. *vivió*
9. *comió*

10. *habló*
11. A
12. C
13. C
14. A
15. A
16. *Son las ocho y cuarenta de la mañana.*
17. *Son las diez y cuarto de la noche.*
18. *Son las nueve y media de la mañana.*
19. *Son las tres menos cuarto de la tarde.*
20. *Son las cuatro y veinte de la tarde.*

Appendix B
Scope and Sequence

Module Scope

These tables detail the scope and sequence of language material for each module of the course.

Module 1

Grammar	Content
Basic nouns	Spanish-speaking countries
Present tense verbs	Common greetings and phrases
Conjugating verbs in the present tense	Animal-related vocabulary
Descriptive adjectives	Spanish names
Elements of a sentence: subjects, verbs, ending phrases	Colors
Creating sentences	Listening and reading comprehension
	Vocabulary-building stories
	Farm-related vocabulary
	Songs using vocabulary words
	Pictographs
	Application of verbs and vocabulary
	Pronunciation practice
	Numbers
	Self quizzes
	Cultural information
	Section assessments

Module 2

Grammar	Content
More present tense verbs	Vocabulary-building stories
Conjugating verbs in the present tense	Vocabulary related to workers and workplaces

Module 2 (cont.)

Grammar	Content
Subjects, verbs, and ending phrases	Library-related vocabulary
When to use *tú* and *usted*	Useful words and phrases
Conjugating verbs in the *tú* and *usted* forms	School-related vocabulary
Talking about the future: "*ir + a*"	Pictographs
	Work-related vocabulary
	Restaurant-related vocabulary
	Telephone greetings and phrases
	More numbers
	Telling time
	Application of verbs and vocabulary
	Self quizzes
	Cultural information
	Section assessments

Module 3

Grammar	Content
Review of "*ir + a*"	Vocabulary related to daily activities
Reflexive verb forms	Listening comprehension practice
Sentence elements: subjects, verbs, adjectives, places	Snack/food-related vocabulary
Creating sentences	Vocabulary-building stories
More present tense verbs	Reading and pronunciation practice
Past tense verbs	Pictographs
	More useful words and phrases
	Review phone conversations and telling time
	Application of verbs and vocabulary
	Self quizzes
	Cultural information
	Section assessments

Course Objectives

Activity 1
→ Read about several reasons for learning Spanish.

Activity 2
→ Learn about Spanish-speaking countries.

Activity 3
→ Listen to and practice saying Spanish greetings and phrases.

Activity 4
→ Learn to identify the Spanish names of animals.

Activity 5
→ Recognize the differences between English and Spanish names.

Activity 6
→ Test your knowledge of animals and verbs.

Activity 7
→ Learn how to use descriptive adjectives.

Activity 8
→ Understand the Spanish words and phrases in the story of "The Little Red Hen."

Activity 9
→ Read about animals living in Spanish-speaking countries.

Activity 10
→ Improve your reading and listening comprehension skills with a very short story.
→ Improve your translation skills by writing the English equivalents of several Spanish animal names and answering questions about different animals.
→ Improve your Spanish vocabulary by matching animals with the Spanish adjectives that describe them.

Activity 11
→ Improve your Spanish vocabulary by learning farm-related words.
→ Learn a song about the animals that live on a farm.

Activity 12
→ Learn about farms in other countries.
→ Improve your Spanish vocabulary by learning more farm-related words.

Activity 13
→ Improve your Spanish vocabulary with nouns, verbs, pronouns, and conjunctions from a story.
→ Check your reading comprehension with questions based on a story.

Activity 14
→ Improve your grammar skills by learning about present tense verbs in Spanish.
→ Improve your writing skills by creating present-tense Spanish sentences of your own.

Activity 15
→ Improve your reading and listening comprehension skills with two very short stories.
→ Master new Spanish vocabulary with match-and-learn squares.

Activity 16
→ Improve your writing skills by describing what your farm would be like, using the farm- and animal-related vocabulary you have studied.

Activity 17
→ Learn to use the Spanish numbers from 1–20.
→ Learn a new song about numbers and dogs.

Activity 18
→ Learn about the music and dances of Spanish-speaking countries.

Activity 19
→ Practice your writing skills and review what you've learned about animals and farms.
→ Read and listen to a short passage, then answer questions on it.

Activity 20
→ Improve your Spanish vocabulary by learning about different workplaces and jobs.

Activity 21
→ Improve your Spanish conversational skills and vocabulary by learning how to describe different occupations in Spanish.

Activity 22
→ Improve your Spanish conversation skills and vocabulary by studying a short passage on the library, then learning phrases that help you interact politely with Spanish-speaking people.

Activity 23
→ Learn about employment situations in Spanish-speaking countries.

Activity 24
→ Improve your Spanish vocabulary and storytelling skills with the third part of the story of the Little Red Hen.

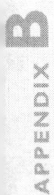

APPENDIX B: SCOPE AND SEQUENCE • COURSE OBJECTIVES

Activity 25
- Solidify your mastery of work-related vocabulary.
- Learn to build correct questions and statements in Spanish.

Activity 26
- Improve your Spanish listening comprehension and reading skills with a short passage and related questions.

Activity 27
- Use the Spanish vocabulary and grammar skills you have acquired so far to write your own short story.

Activity 28
- Learn to describe what people of different professions are doing in Spanish.
- Improve your Spanish speaking skills by learning about telephone conversations in Spanish.

Activity 29
- Master different telephone conversations in Spanish.

Activity 30
- Review the Spanish numbers 1–20.
- Learn the Spanish numbers 21–69.
- Learn simple time telling in Spanish.

Activity 31
- Improve your reading, listening, and conversation skills through more telephone conversation practice.

Activity 32
- Increase your Spanish vocabulary and improve your reading and listening skills with a pair of telephone interviews and comprehension materials.

Activity 33
- Learn vocabulary and increase reading comprehension and storytelling skills with the first part of a DiglotWeave™ story.

Activity 34
- Improve Spanish grammar skills by learning how to discuss the future in Spanish.
- Practice what you've learned with listening comprehension passages and matching activities.

Activity 35
- Consolidate what you've learned by writing a telephone conversation in Spanish.

Activity 36
- Improve your reading and listening comprehension skills with a passage entirely in Spanish.

Activity 37
- Learn to apply what you learned about future tense to what you learned about telephone conversations.

Activity 38
- Improve your vocabulary and conversation skills by learning to discuss your daily routine in Spanish.

Activity 39
- Answer questions about vocabulary you have learned.
- Learn a fun game to practice your Spanish vocabulary.

Activity 40
- Learn how to use reflexive verbs in Spanish.

Activity 41
- Increase your Spanish vocabulary and build your listening and reading comprehension skills with the second part of this DiglotWeave™ story.

Activity 42
- Learn to compare daily life in the US with daily life in some Spanish-speaking countries.

Activity 43
- Improve your writing skills and solidify your grammar and vocabulary skills by writing in Spanish about a day in your life.

Activity 44
- Learn more about reflexive verbs in Spanish.

Activity 45
- Make posters, using Spanish vocabulary you have learned, that show what you do at different times of the day.

Activity 46
- Practice your translation skills.
- Learn a Spanish saying and two new phrases.

Activity 47
- Learn about foods in different Spanish-speaking countries.
- Master meal-related vocabulary in Spanish.

Activity 48
- Increase your Spanish vocabulary and storytelling skills with this DiglotWeave™ story.

Activity 49
- Learn the phrases and grammar you would need to plan a trip to a farm.

Activity 50
- Improve your reading and listening comprehension skills and increase your Spanish vocabulary using a passage describing Mario's farm.

Activity 51
→ Improve your Spanish grammar by learning about the past tense of regular Spanish verbs.
→ Write a postcard to practice what you have learned.

Activity 52
→ Learn about the Mexican holiday *Cinco de Mayo*.
→ Develop your Spanish writing skills by writing about some of the holidays you celebrate.

Activity 53
→ Hone your Spanish grammar skills by learning more about Spanish past tense.

Activity 54
→ Solidify what you have learned about phone conversations, telling time, past tense verbs, and foods.

Appendix C
Index of Marginalia

Introduction

Culture facts and other interesting information can be found in the margins throughout the course. While not part of your course curriculum, these marginalia provide a fun and educational view into the many exciting facets of Spanish-speaking regions.

Index

Refrán, page 14.
¿Sabías qué...?—**Did you know...?,** page 16.
Refrán, page 54.
Maracas, page 84.
Refrán, page 96.
Little Shops, page 99.
Refrán, page 180.
La Zona Rosa, page 197.
Refrán, page 215.
Bananas and Eggs, page 217.
Churros, page 218.
Arroz con leche, page 219.
Papel picado, page 236.
Make a *piñata,* page 239.
Make *papel picado,* page 240.
Piñatas, page 241.

Culture Notes

As you've worked through the course, you may have been interested in certain countries or interesting facts and histories. Write any notes about people, places, or things that you would like do more research on.

APPENDIX C : INDEX OF MARGINALIA • CULTURE NOTES

APPENDIX C : INDEX OF MARGINALIA • CULTURE NOTES